GREAT BEERS

GREAT BEERS

THE BEST BEERS FROM AROUND THE WORLD

Editor-in-chief **TIM HAMPSON**

Penguin Random House

Edited by Elizabeth Yeates
Designed by Alison Shackleton
Senior Jacket Creative Mark Penfound
Pre-Production Producer Andy Hilliard
Senior Producer Verity Powell
Special Sales Creative Project Manager Alison Donovan

First published in 2010
This updated edition first published 2014
by DK Publishing
345 Hudson Street, New York, New York 10014

Material first published in the United States in 2008
in *The Beer Book*

Copyright © 2008, 2010, 2014 Dorling Kindersley Limited
DK, a Division of Penguin Random House LLC

16 17 18 19 10 9 8 7 6 5 4 3 2 1
001—274442—Jul/2014

A catalog record for this book is available from
the Library of Congress

ISBN 978-1-4654-3356-5

Color reproduction by Colourscan, Singapore

Printed and bound in China by Hung Hing Printing Co. Ltd.

A WORLD OF IDEAS
SEE ALL THERE IS TO KNOW
www.dk.com

Contents

Introduction

This book is an adventure—a journey through a fascinating world of flavors, colors, and aromas. These pages constitute a trip around the world in ales, porters, and pilsners, and an introduction to the master brewers behind the world's greatest drink.

These are exciting times for beer lovers. With the US leading the way in terms of innovation, in the last few decades brewers have been pushing at boundaries as never before. From Alaska to the Mexican border, America's craft brewers are brewing darker beers, bitterer beers, and hoppier beers than can be found anywhere else in the world. European beer styles are being taken apart and put back together with barely a nod to tradition. In brewing terms, there are simply no rules anymore.

Meanwhile, the great brewing nations of Europe—Germany, Belgium, the Czech Republic—still stand tall, with glorious tradition standing alongside intriguing innovation. Countries historically associated more with grape than grain are also making great strides—Italy's brewers are among the most experimental and ambitious worldwide, and their efforts have been yielding remarkable results.

The other good news for lovers of great beer is that it has never been easier for drinkers to sample such a wide range of beers from around the world. A trip to your local shop or supermarket will in most cases provide a selection of several of the brews featured in this book. More ambitious readers may be encouraged to travel further to track down exciting tipples and experience the brewing and drinking culture of some of the world's top beer destinations. If this appeals to you, this book introduces tours of Oregon, Brussels, the Cotswolds, Prague, and Bamberg—range of destinations representing the best of the old and new worlds of beer.

This book is intended for people who want to broaden their knowledge of beer and hunt down exciting brews from around the globe. It should encourage you never to ask just for a beer without first considering its style—pilsner or wheat, fruit or an American IPA, Belgian ale or a gueuze? For there can be few better pleasures—when returning home after a long day at work or just sitting in a favorite bar—than the pleasure of a great beer. But which one? The choice is yours—enjoy the experience.

Tim Hampson

A

Aass Bryggeri

NORWAY

Postboks 1530,
N-3007 Drammen,
www.aass.no

Norway's oldest brewery dates back to
1834. Named after Poul Lauritz Aass
(pronounced "ouse"), it is a family-
owned business run by four
generations since 1860.

BREWING SECRET Aass brews
according to the strict 1516
Bavarian Law of Purity, drawing
its water from the nearby lake
of Glitre.

Aass Bock
DUNKLER BOCK 6.5% ABV
Smooth and creamy; brewed using
Munich malt and Hallertau hops.
Lagered for at least three months.

Aass Juleøl
DUNKLER BOCK 6.2% ABV
The most sought-after Christmas
beer in Scandinavia. Thick and
malty with a smooth, rich flavor.

Abbaye des Rocs

BELGIUM

37, Chaussée Brunehault, B7387
Montignies-sur-Roc,
www.abbaye-des-rocs.com

Jean-Pierre Eloir, a former exciseman,
took up brewing in 1979. The business
has since expanded, with the beers
gaining a good reputation, particularly
abroad, and some are now being
developed with export in mind.

BREWING SECRET Core beers are
true to the spiced and well-bodied
Walloon style; keg beers are often
unfiltered.

Blanche des Honnelles
WITBIER 6% ABV
Not your usual wheat beer, this one
is made from malted barley, malted
wheat, and home-malted oats.

Abbaye des Rocs Brune
BELGIAN DARK STRONG ALE 9% ABV
Very spiced and sustaining, with a
nourishing touch. Well-liked in
Anglo-Saxon countries.

9

Achelse Kluis

BELGIUM

De Kluis 1,
B3930 Hamont-Achel,
www.achelsekluis.org

At a time when there were many
brewery closures, the Belgian beer
world had cause to celebrate in 1998.
That was when De Achelse Kluis—a
Trappist abbey on the Dutch border—
started up brewing again after 84
unproductive years! It is run as a
pub-brewery, and draws in many
passing walkers and cyclists.

Achel Bruin 8
TRAPPIST BEER 8% ABV
More than the draft beers on tap,
this is a classic Trappist brew;
heavy, estery, and filling.

Achel Extra Bruin
DARK TRAPPIST 9.5% ABV
The flagship of brewmaster
Knops—who refuses to drink
anything else—rich and rewarding.

Acorn

ENGLAND

Wombwell, Barnsley,
South Yorkshire, S73 8HA
www.acornbrewery.net

One of the newer microbreweries in
England, Acorn was set up in 2003
and doubled capacity in its first four
years. It now produces 40 barrels
(6,500 liters) every week.

BREWING SECRET The yeast
strain from the 1850s Barnsley
Brewery has been reintroduced,
coinciding with the company
gathering significant awards.

Barnsley Bitter
BITTER 3.8% ABV
Ripe chestnut in color, with
a rounded, rich flavor that
lingers in the bitter finish.

Barnsley Gold
STRONG BITTER 4.3% ABV
Beautifully golden, with citrus
fruit hop aromas orchestrating the
ensemble through to its dry finish.

Adnams

ENGLAND

Southwold, Suffolk, IP18 6JW
www.adnams.co.uk

Its "Beers from the Coast" have been brewed in the classic English seaside town of Southwold since 1872. In recent years, technological innovation has driven refurbishment, while an emphasis on traditional methods has been studiously maintained. An eco-friendly distribution center—complete with living grass roof—summarizes the dynamic approach.

Adnams Broadsidee
STRONG BITTER **4.7**% ABV
Rich, fruitcake aromas dominate initially, giving way to an elegant hop and malt association.

Adnams Bitter
BITTER **3.7**% ABV
Aromatic hop and biscuit malt fragrances introduce a lingering, dry, and refreshingly bitter flavor.

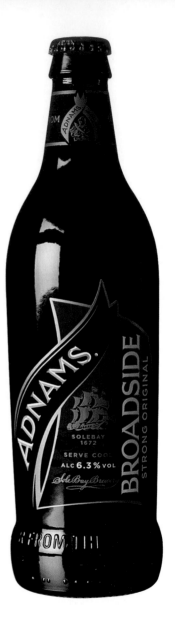

Airbräu

GERMANY

Münchner Airportcenter,
Terminalstr. Mitte 18, 85356 München,
www.allresto.de

This brewery has a unique location: set
between the two terminals of Munich
airport. It opened in 2004 at the same
time as the airport's new Terminal 2,
and it includes a much-frequented
restaurant and beer garden. Two
brewing kettles are situated right in
the middle of the restaurant.

Fliegerquell
LAGER 5.2% ABV
Deep golden, finely structured,
and classically dry. It is brewed
for international palates.

Kumulus
WHITE BEER 5.4% ABV
Typical yellow color; a sparkling,
very fresh white beer, refreshing
and full-bodied.

Aktien

GERMANY

Hohe Buchleute 3, 87600 Kaufbeuren,
www.aktienbrauerei.de

The origins of brewing at the Aktien
brewery in Kaufbeuren can be traced
back to the early 14th century. In
more recent times, Aktien has taken
over the Löwen and Rosen breweries.

BREWING SECRET Aktien still
brews its beer strictly according
to the Bavarian Purity Law set
in 1516.

Naturtrübes Kellerbier
KELLERBIER 5.1% ABV
Unfiltered and naturally cloudy
out of the cellar. The slightly
sweet taste is typical of one of
the oldest styles of beer in Bavaria.

Fendt Dieselrossöl
MÄRZEN 5.9% ABV
A malty, aromatic structure and
a full-bodied, slightly bitter taste.
Goes well with venison dishes.

Alaskan

USA

5429 Shaune Drive
Juneau, AK 99801,
www.alaskanbeer.com

Although it is located in a coastal Alaska community cut off from the lower 48, Alaskan Brewing has grown into a force that spreads from the western coast of Canada down through much of the US west of the Rockies. Founders Geoff and Marcy Larson focused on native ingredients and recipes from the outset. Alaskan's first and flagship brew, Amber Ale, is based on a beer made across the channel from Juneau back at the turn of the 20th century.

Amber
ALTBIER 5% ABV
Clean caramel on the nose, brightened by spicy hops. Smooth and malty, with balanced bitterness.

Barley Wine Ale
BARLEY WINE 10.4% ABV
Cellared in a former gold mine. Rich and smooth, with dark caramel, cherries, and plums. Nicely balanced.

15

Alesmith

USA

9368 Cabot Drive
San Diego, CA 92126,
www.alesmith.com

One of several San Diego breweries
that has pushed Southern California
to the forefront of national brewing.
It has a wide following for its mostly
strong and often esoteric beers, many
barrel-aged and vintage-dated.

BREWING SECRET Every
employee is an award-winning
home brewer.

Speedway Stout
IMPERIAL STOUT 12% ABV
It's coffee-infused, complementing
a broad imperial palate of
chocolate, toffee, currants,
and oily nuts.

IPA
INDIA PALE ALE 7.3% ABV
Brimming with hops and fruit
salad aromas, including notes
of ripe mango and pineapple.

Alhambra

SPAIN

Avenida de Murcia 1,
18012 Granada,
www.cervezasalhambra.com

The Alhambra group was founded in 1925 and is named after Granada's famed Moorish palace. Spain's purest water comes from the nearby Sierra Nevada mountain range, and is used in the making of Alhambra beers.

BREWING SECRET The brewery uses traditional techniques that include fermentation lasting up to 39 days.

Alhambra Premium
LAGER 4.6% ABV
A soft gold in color, its nose is lemony and fresh with a hint of malt. A well-balanced, quaffable beer.

Mezquita
WHEAT BEER 7.2% ABV
A full-bodied, assertive red wheat beer with caramel notes and hints of pepper in the aroma.

Allagash

USA

100 Industrial Way
Portland, ME 04103,
www.allagash.com

Focusing on Belgian-inspired beers,
Allagash draws on tradition but does
not shy away from innovation. In 2007
it became the first American brewery to
build a traditional "coolship" (a huge,
open, shallow pan) for spontaneous
fermentation by wild yeasts.

BREWING SECRET Some specialty
beers are aged in oak bourbon barrels.

Allagash White
WITBIER 6.2% ABV
Appropriately cloudy, fruity, and
refreshing. Brightened by subtle
coriander and Curaçao orange peel.

Curieux
TRIPLE 10% ABV
Allagash Tripel ale, aged in Jim Beam
barrels. Orchard fruits and honey
meet bourbon, vanilla, and wood.

Allersheim

GERMANY

Allersheim 6, 37603 Holzminden,
www.brauerei-allersheim.de

Founded in 1854, this brewery was,
for Otto Baumgarten, merely a sideline
to farming. He harvested the grain in
his own fields, but had to buy in the
hops. Production grew over the years,
though, and today the brewery has
40 employees.

BREWING SECRET The beers
are brewed to suit discerning
local palates.

Landbier
PILSNER 5% ABV
A pilsner with a mash bill from
light and dark malt. Soft in taste,
with a typical malty aroma.

Blue Moon
BEER AND COLA 1.9% ABV
A pleasant mix of dry hops and
cola. It's not too sweet, because the
mix is produced without sugar.

Alpirsbach

GERMANY

Alpirsbacher Klosterbräu, Marktplatz 1,
72275 Alpirsbach,
www.alpirsbacher.de

A railroad was constructed through
the Black Forest at the end of the 19th
century, which brought many visitors
to the village of Alpirsbach. Johann
Gottfried Glauner helped to cater for
them by reopening the old village
brewery. Sales were good, and today
the beer from Alpirsbach is produced
by the fourth generation of the family.

Kleiner Mönch
LAGER 5.2% ABV
The golden color promises a fresh,
young beer. It is full-bodied with a
flavor of caramel from the malt.

Schwarzes Pils
PILSNER 4.9% ABV
Deep red-black color and a strong
taste, with a roasted malt aroma
that is unmistakable.

Altöttinger

GERMANY

Altöttinger Hell-Brau,
Herrenmühlstr. 15, 84503 Altötting,
www.altoettinger-hellbraeu.de

The Bavarian town of Altötting is
home to the Altötting Madonna, a
world-famous pilgrimage site. In
1890 Georg Hell expanded production
at a local brewery to help cater to
thirsty pilgrims. Today the brewery
produces eight different beers.

BREWING SECRET The finest
hops and best German malts
are used.

Bayerische Dunkel
DUNKEL 5.2% ABV
Roasty and malty taste, but fresh,
and with a long finish. A dark
specialty with its own character.

Fein-Herb
LAGER 5% ABV
The best malts, combined with a
careful selection of hops, produce
an exceptionally dry, fine taste.

Amsterdam Brewing

CANADA

21 Bathurst Street, Toronto,
Ontario, M5V 2NG,
www.amsterdambeer.com

Purity, passion, and revelry are the
watchwords for Toronto's first brewpub.
Founded in 1986, it was an immediate
success. Business was brisk, and it soon
moved to another site before finding its
current home in 2005. The brewery stands
opposite the historic Fort York, the 1793
birthplace of modern Toronto. In 2003,
when the Kawartha Lakes Brewing
Company closed, its brands were sold
to Amsterdam Brewing.

KLB Nut Brown Ale
BROWN ALE 5% ABV
The unmistakable tang of East Kent
Golding hops. Sweet to taste, it has
hints of honey and chocolate.

Amsterdam Wheat Beer
WHEAT BEER 4% ABV
Light in color, with malt sweetness
and a hint of fresh bread. Often
served chilled with a slice of lemon.

Anchor

USA

705 Mariposa St.
San Francisco, CA 94107,
www.anchorbrewing.com

Fritz Maytag saved Anchor Brewing
from closing in 1965, introduced US
drinkers to many classic styles, and
launched a microbrewery revolution.

BREWING SECRET Maytag
is known for preserving the
indigenous "steam style," which
involves using bottom-fermenting
yeast at high temperatures in
wide, shallow, open pans.

Liberty Ale
PALE ALE 6% ABV
A benchmark American pale ale.
Fruity and floral on the nose;
crisp bitterness on the palate.

Anchor Steam
STEAM BEER 4.9% ABV
A signature woody, minty nose.
Well-rounded caramel flavors
yield to a firm, crisp finish.

23

Andechs

GERMANY

Kloster Andechs, Bergstr. 2,
82346 Andechs,
www.andechs.de

The Benedictine monks of Andechs
began to produce beer in 1455. The
monastery updated its brewery in
1972, investing in modern equipment.
Still closely associated with the holy
mountain pilgrimage site southwest
of Munich, Andechs today is a brand
name that's internationally known.

Bergbock Hell
BOCK 7% ABV
A strong beer, but it tastes mild and
aromatic. Its typical light sweetness
gives it a full body.

Doppelbock Dunkel
BOCK 7% ABV
This world-famous beer has a really
strong taste. The dark malts give it
an unmistakable character, with a
light aroma of hops in the finish.

Anderson Valley

USA

17700 Highway 253
Boonville, CA 95415,
www.avbc.com

Set in Mendocino County's picturesque
Anderson Valley, this solar-powered
brewery mixes local and international
styles and techniques. Some beer names
are those of local landmarks, others are
in Boontling, a regional dialect.

BREWING SECRET The copper
brew kettles were rescued from
a closed-down German brewery.

Boont ESB
EXTRA SPECIAL BITTER 6.8% ABV
Citrussy hops layer fruit on top of
bready malt. Tangy in the middle;
a long and mildly bitter finish.

Barney Flats Oatmeal Stout
OATMEAL STOUT 5.7% ABV
Impression of coffee and cream,
sweetness balanced by roasted
grains, the complexity heightened
by earthy undertones.

Anheuser-Busch

USA

One Busch Plaza
St. Louis, MO 63119,
www.anheuser-busch.com

Anheuser-Busch brews half the beer
sold in the United States, including
Budweiser and Bud Light, two of the
world's best-selling brands. With its
Michelob line, seasonal specialties,
and beers produced by its regional
breweries for local consumers, the
company has significantly broadened
the range of its beers.

Michelob
MALT LAGER 5% ABV
Returned to its all-malt roots
in 2007. Delicate, with a spicy
nose, clean malt middle and
crisp, dry finish.

Stone Mill Organic Pale Ale
PALE ALE 5.5% ABV
Organic beer under the Green Valley
Brewing label. This ale is lightly
bready with earthy hop character.

Anker

BELGIUM

uido Gezellelaan 49,
B2800 Mechelen,
www.hetanker.be

Now here's a brewery with a history.
The owners claim it began in 1369,
but it was in 1873 that the Van
Breedam family took over and began
its modern brewing age. In the 1990s,
the end for the classic Gouden Carolus
seemed near, but a family buy-out from
the ill-fated RIVA empire succeeded,
and now the brewery is productive
and innovative once more.

Gouden Carolus Classic
STRONG DARK ALE 8.5% ABV
This malt bomb has a
characteristic taste of raisins in
portwine. An exemplary strong,
dark Belgian ale.

Gouden Carolus Christmas
STRONG DARK ALE 10.5% ABV
The raisins and molasses from
the Carolus Classic are present,
but with a greater alcohol kick.

27

Ankerbräu Nordlingen

GERMANY

Ankergasse 4, 86720 Nördlingen,
www.ankerbrauerei.de

The brewery's history can be traced from
1608, when several beers were brewed here
for a festival. It was acquired by the Grandel
family at the end of the 19th century.

BREWING SECRET The beers
are made with local malts, mineral
water from the Ries, and hops
from Spalt.

Lager Hell
LAGER 5% ABV
A full-flavored clear, yellow beer;
pleasant and full-bodied, with
a fine aroma at the beginning.

Nördlinger Premium Pils
PILSNER 4.7% ABV
A very flowery hop aroma
turns slightly bitter and a
bit sparkling on the tongue.

Antares

ARGENTINA

17 Esquina 71, La Plata - P de Bs As, 7600,
www.cervezaantares.com.ar

Antares is the brightest star in the
Scorpius constellation, and the brewpub
that shares its name sparkles too.
Stylish and smart, it offers a lively
alternative to beers from international
brewers. Brews include a kölsch, a
Scotch ale, a honey beer, a cream stout,
a barley wine, and an imperial stout,
with some variations in style.

Antares Stout Imperial
IMPERIAL STOUT 8.5% ABV
Intense liquorice and toasted
flavors give way to roasted
coffee and caramelized orange
intensities.

Antares Kölsch
KÖLSCH 5% ABV
A well hopped and highly
drinkable ale style. Good
fruity overtones make it
an ideal partner to food.

Arcadia

USA

103 West Michigan Avenue
Battle Creek, MI 49017,
www.arcadiabrewingcompany.com

Using the British Peter Austin system
more common in the Northeast, and
brewing with British malts, Arcadia
leans toward UK-inspired ales, but
made with citrussy and piney Pacific
Northwest hops. Ringwood yeast gives
the beers a fresh character, and they
work particularly well on cask.

London Porter
PORTER 7.2% ABV
Rich on the nose, flavors of coffee
beans, chocolate, and dark fruit,
with a lingering, dessertlike finish.

Scotch Ale
SCOTTISH ALE 7.5% ABV
Nuttiness and piney hops don't
totally balance here. The final
impression is of sweet caramel.

Arco

GERMANY

Schlossallee 1, 94554 Moos,
www.arcobraeu.de

Arco has been owned by the Counts
of Arco-Zinneberg for 450 years.
The castle and brewery belonging
to the family are situated in Moos, a
small town in the heart of Niederbayern
in Bavaria, where the rivers Isar and
Donau converge. The current Count
Arco personally launched the beers
in the US in 2004.

Schloss Hell
LAGER 4.9% ABV
With its soft but full-bodied taste
and golden color, Arco's Schloss
Hell typifies Bavarian lager.

Urfass
LAGER 5.2% ABV
Slightly more bitter than the Schloss
Hell, and especially spicy, this is a
real premium lager of Bavaria.

31

Asia Pacific Breweries

SINGAPORE

459 Jalan Ahmad Ibrahim,
639934
www.tigerbeer.com

Widely available across Asia, AP's beers are
now brewed in seven different countries.
Tiger Beer—its most famous—was first
produced in the 1930s, when the "Time
for a Tiger" slogan was first used. Anthony
Burgess named the first novel in his The
Long Day Wanes trilogy *Time for a Tiger*.

Tiger
LAGER 5% ABV
A golden colored refreshing
lager. It is normally served
so chilled that its taste and
aromas are masked.

ABC Extra Stout
STOUT 8% ABV
A strong but easy-drinking beer.
The nose is robust, with roasted
coffee and chocolate flavors.

Auer

GERMANY

Münchner Str. 80, 83022 Rosenheim,
www.auerbraeu.de

Between 1887 and 1920, Johann Auer
acquired several plots of land and
some breweries around the town
of Rosenheim, southeast of Munich.
Since then, the company has
expanded considerably.

BREWING SECRET When it was
founded, this was one of the most
modern breweries in Bavaria.

Bajuware Dunkel
DUNKEL 5.5% ABV
Brewed in old-fashioned Bavarian
style, this beer has a malty aroma
and a full-bodied character.

Weizenbock
WHEAT BOCK 7% ABV
A strong, spicy specialty. A good
accompaniment to hearty cheeses
or sweet desserts.

Augustiner

GERMANY

Landsberger Str. 31-35, 80339 München,
www.augustiner-braeu.de

Founded in 1328, this is the oldest
brewery in Munich and one of only
two in the city (along with Hofbräu
München) that do not belong to a giant
of the global brewing industry. The site
as it is today was constructed in 1885.
Augustiner beer has become famous
around the world even though the
brewery does not advertise itself.

Edelstoff
EXPORT 5.6% ABV
The unusual dark golden color
displays its special character.
A sweet and obvious hop taste
guides you to a very malty finish.

Weissbier
WHEAT BEER 5.4% ABV
Golden and cloudy, this is a
full-bodied wheat beer with a citrus
taste and light bitters in the finish.

August Schell

USA

1860 Schell Road
New Ulm, MN 56073,
www.schellsbrewery.com

Family-owned since August Schell founded it in 1860, this brewery has perhaps the most beautiful setting in the US, with ornamental gardens and a former carriage house converted into a museum. In 2002 the company took over production of the legendary Grain Belt Premium beer, when that brewery failed, to save a Minnesota icon from extinction.

Caramel Bock
BOCK 5.6% ABV
Rich caramel on the nose, turning rummy on the palate. Sweetness lingers after a not-quite dry finish.

Schmaltz Alt
ALTBIER 5% ABV
Subtle combination of biscuit and chocolate balanced by mild, slightly spicy hop flavors and bitterness.

Au in der Hallertau

GERMANY

Schlossbrauerei Au in der Hallertau,
Schlossbräugasse 2, 84072 Au,
www.auer-bier.de

Au is at the heart of the largest hop-growing area in the world. It was linked with the master brewer Schweiger in 1590 and, since 1846, has been owned by six generations of the Earls Beck of Peccoz. A modern approach is an essential feature of the management at Au in der Hallertau.

Hopfengold
EXPORT 5% ABV
Golden color, full-bodied taste with fine bitters of hops and clear malt. Nice finish, not too sweet.

Holledauer Leichtes
WHEAT BEER 3.3% ABV
A cloudy yellow, light wheat beer, fresh and lightly sparkling; not too heavy a taste, and with a slightly bitter finish.

Avery

USA

5763 Arapahoe Avenue
Boulder, CO 80803,
www.averybrewing.com

Located near the Rocky Mountains,
though in a nondescript industrial
park, this brewery has earned a
reputation for its hoppy beers and
its astonishingly strong beers
(sometimes they are both). These
include a threesome nicknamed the
"Demons of Ale," in which the beers
average 15 percent ABV apiece.

India Pale Ale
INDIA PALE ALE 6.3% ABV
Piney, oily nose, with grapefruit
and orange from the aroma to
the palate. Unapologetically bitter.

Salvation
BELGIAN STRONG GOLDEN ALE 9% ABV
Fleshy fruits, particularly apricots,
mingle with sweet, spicy aromas
and flavors, and a surprising
hint of honey.

37

Ayinger

GERMANY

Zornedinger Str. 1,
85653 Aying,
www.ayinger.de

Johann Liebhard founded this brewery
in Aying in 1876, at a time when there
were about 6,000 breweries in Bavaria.
That number has dropped to about 700
today, but Ayinger has survived and
was renovated by the Inselkammer
family in 1999. It has since become
more widely known.

Jahrhundertbier
EXPORT 5.5% ABV
A honeylike aroma with light
flowery hops leads on to a
harmonious finish.

Celebrator
DOPPELBOCK 6.7% ABV
The taste of malt dominates this
nearly black, strong beer. It is
not as sweet as other doppelbocks
of the same quality.

Barley

ITALY

Via C. Colombo, 09040 Maracalagonis (CA),
Sardinia,
www.barley.it

Skilful home brewer Nicola Perra
established this microbrewery in 2006
in southern Sardinia, challenging
the mass-market lagers so popular
in the region (consumption here is
the highest in Italy).

BREWING SECRET Local
ingredients such as Sardinian
wine wort and organic honey
are used in the ales.

Toccadibò
GOLDEN STRONG ALE 8.4% ABV
A warming ale; spicy, hoppy
and dry, with intriguing bitter-
almond notes of amaretto.

BB 10
BARLEY WINE 10% ABV
A unique brew made with *sapa*, the
boiled wort of local Cannonau grapes.
A highly distinctive nightcap.

39

Barons

AUSTRALIA

1 Moncur Street, Woollahra,
New South Wales 2025,
www.baronsbrewing.com

"Beer barons" by name and nature,
this relative newcomer has its brands
produced under contract and is one of
the country's fastest-growing craft beer
players; they are also eyeing export
markets in the US and Russia.

BREWING SECRET Barons makes
use of indigenous "bush tucker"
ingredients, such as wattle seed
and lemon myrtle.

Lemon Myrtle Witbier
BELGIAN WITBIER 5% ABV
Moderate carbonation, lime-scented
mid-palate with spicy hints,
followed by a clean, crisp finish.

Black Wattle Original Ale
SPICED AMBER ALE 5.8% ABV
Creamy mouthfeel, malt-driven,
with hints of roasted nuts,
chocolate, and milky coffee.

Bateman

ENGLAND

Wainfleet, Lincolnshire,
PE24 4JE
www.bateman.co.uk

One of the country's oldest and most
picturesque family breweries—with
a windmill towering high above—it
has a well-deserved reputation for
"good honest ales." A family split
almost destroyed the business in
the 1980s, but it survived, blossomed,
and has developed a new brewhouse
and engaging visitor center.

XXXB
STRONG BITTER 4.8% ABV
Classic russet-tan ale, with
a well constructed blend of
malt, hops, and fruitiness.

XB Bitter
BITTER 3.7% ABV
Finely balanced, with an apple-
influenced hop aroma that
lingers alongside the malty flavor.

Bath Ales

ENGLAND

Warmley, Bristol,
BS30 8XN
www.bathales.com

The founders' brewing backgrounds
and insistence on traditional methods
operating alongside cutting-edge
technology has resulted in Bath Ale's
reputation for distinctive, characterful,
and flavorsome ales. The success of the
business has led to the brewery twice
outgrowing its premises since it was
established in 1995. A bottling plant
and shop continue the growth.

Gem Bitter
BEST BITTER **4.1**% ABV
Rich and full-textured, with
a malt, fruit, and bitter-sweet
hop quality throughout.

Special Pale Ale (SPA)
PALE ALE **3.7**% ABV
A prominent hop aroma and bitter
malty touch complement its
light-bodied character.

Bathams

ENGLAND

Brierley Hill, West Midlands,
DY5 2TN
www.bathams.com

The brewery's frontage—actually the Vine Inn—is emblazoned with a quotation from Shakespeare's *Two Gentlemen of Verona*: "Blessing of you: You brew good ale." Five generations of the Batham family have been involved since the brewery was established in 1877, each nurturing its reputation for classic Black Country mild ales.

Bathams Best Bitter
BEST BITTER 4.5% ABV
Straw-colored ale, with an initial sweetness, soon overtaken by a complex, dry, hoppy flavor.

Bathams Mild Ale
MILD 3.5% ABV
A fruity, dark brown mild; sweet and well-balanced, with a hoppy fruit finish.

43

Bavik

BELGIUM

Rijksweg 33,
B-8531 Bavikhove Harelbeke,
www.bavik.be

With the fourth generation of the
De Brabandere family, this brewery
is run efficiently and encompasses
a large number of tied pubs too.

BREWING SECRET Abbey ales
and pilsners form an important
role in the annual output (especially
to supermarkets), but the most
interesting brews are in the
oud bruin tradition.

Petrus Oud Bruin (Dark)
OUD BRUIN **5.5% ABV**
Recently, the brewery invested
in giant wooden barrels for
fermenting this vinous,
quite traditional ale.

Petrus Aged Pale
OUD BRUIN **7.3% ABV**
In the new barrels, you'll find this:
the undiluted pale beer, ageing for
years, gaining sourish, fruity notes.

44

Bayern Meister Bier

JAPAN

1254-1 Kawaharabata,
Inouede-aza, Fujinomiya City,
Shizuoka 418-0103,
www.bmbier.com

Brewmaster Stefan Rager originally
came to Japan to brew at several start-up
microbreweries which opened after the
1995 liberalization. Later, with his
Japanese wife, he founded a boutique-
style brewery on the southern face of
Mount Fuji, dedicated to German beer
styles. The German Embassy in Tokyo
is one of his most loyal customers.

Prinz Pils
PILSNER 5.5% ABV
Pale yellow, soft mouthfeel
with low carbonation. The subtle
flavors are in excellent balance.

Amadeus Doppelbock
DOPPELBOCK 8% ABV
Very deep reddish brown, with
coffee, toffee, and caramel aromas.
Rich tangy malt and high alcohol
suggest rum-soaked fruitcake.

45

B

Bear Republic

USA

345 Healdsburg Avenue
Healdsburg, CA 95448,
www.bearrepublic.com

With a brewpub located amidst the
Sonoma County wine-tasting rooms
and a brewery north of town, Bear
Republic presents a decidedly different
break for wine tourists. Founding
brewmaster (and fireman and race-car-
driver) Richard Norgrove is just as
skilled as any wine blender when
merging hops flavors and aromas.

Racer 5
INDIA PALE ALE 7% ABV
Delightfully fresh grapefruit and
thick piney aromas, built on a
resinous, malty-sweet middle.

Hop Rod Rye
IMPERIAL INDIA PALE ALE 8% ABV
Bright, citrussy nose with spicy
alcohols. A subtle blend of biscuit
and clean rye. Incessant hops.

Bell's

USA

8938 Krum Avenue
Galesburg, MI 49053,
www.bellsbeer.com

The oldest surviving microbrewery east of Colorado, Bell's (formerly Kalamazoo Brewing) has grown nearly 700-fold since its first sales in 1985. Bell's has built a new brewing facility outside Kalamazoo, but the original brewery remains, along with its appropriately named Eccentric Café. Bell's beers are famous for their intensity, although the brewery flagship is wheat-based.

Expedition Stout
IMPERIAL STOUT 11.5% ABV
Begins with an intense blast of dark fruit (figs and plums) that turns into chocolate, roasted coffee, and port.

Oberon Ale
WHEAT BEER 5.8% ABV
A summer refresher. Zesty, with orange rind in the aroma, and delicate spiciness behind that. A crisp, sharp finish.

Berg

GERMANY

Berg Brauerei Ulrich Zimmermann, Brauhausstr. 2,
89548 Ehingen-Berg,
www.bergbier.de

Berg, founded in 1757, is family-owned and
one of the smallest breweries in Germany.

BREWING SECRET Berg makes
use of corn in brewing, which is
supplied by an organic farm
nearby.

Berg Original
LAGER 4.8% ABV
Its smooth, dry taste makes this
beer the most popular brand
offered by the brewery.

Berg Märzen
MÄRZEN 6.1% ABV
A typical strong beer. The taste
is very hearty, not least because
of its high dose of hops.

48

Bergquell

GERMANY

Weststr. 7, Löbau,
www.bergquell-loebau.de

With its long brewing tradition, the Bergquell Brauerei Löbau has played an important role in the Lausitz region since 1846. It is also one of the most advanced breweries in the whole of Germany and is well known for its wide range of special beers.

BREWING SECRET The special beers have an international following.

Kirsch Porter
PORTER 4.2% ABV
A black beer with a cherry flavor and typical porter qualities. Malty and full-bodied.

Lausitzer Porter
PORTER 4.4% ABV
Typical porter with a dry, roasted malt taste. It is full-bodied and not too heavy; dark colored and a little bit sweet.

Berkshire

12 Railroad Street South
Deerfield, MA 01373,
www.berkshirebrewingcompany.com

Western Massachusetts' local brewery
(although its beers are increasingly
easy to find in Boston). BBC handles
almost all its own distribution,
guaranteeing that its beer will
be fresh and retain a subtle,
balanced complexity that begins
with open fermentation.

BREWING SECRET These
pure, unfiltered beers must
be kept refrigerated.

Drayman's Porter
PORTER 6.2% ABV
Coffeelike aromas, a complex
middle (chocolate and toffee),
and a pleasantly bitter finish.

Raspberry Strong Ale
FRUIT BEER 9% ABV
Brewed with fresh berries and
released for Valentine's Day.
Scarily nicknamed "Truth Serum."

GREAT BEERS

B

50

Berliner Kindl-Schultheiss

GERMANY

Indira-Ghandi-Str. 66-69, 13053 Berlin,
www.berliner-kindl.de

The union of the Berliner Kindl and
Berliner Schultheiss breweries in 2006
was symbolic for Germany, whose
breweries had declined through
post-War division. The merger has
generated a great many new brands,
produced in one of the most modern
brewing facilities in Germany.

Märkischer Landmann
SCHWARZBIER 4.9% ABV
Black and highly malty, but
without any bitterness. A genuine
original of the Märkish region.

Bockbier
BOCK 7% ABV
Golden, strong, and not too sweet;
pleasant, with a smooth finish—
a typical bock.

Bernard

CZECH REPUBLIC

5 Května č.1, 396 01 Humpolec,
www.bernard.cz

While reviving 16th-century Humpolec
brewery in 1991, Stanislav Bernard and
two partners took the daring decision
to produce traditional unpasteurized
beers using microfiltration. Since
then, awards and an expanding
export market have followed.

BREWING SECRET Bernard
has its own floor maltings
and uses spring water.

Celebration / Sváteční Ležák
PREMIUM LAGER 5% ABV
Delicate herblike hop and yeast
aromas overlay a peppery
bitterness for a grassy finish.

Amber / Jantarový Ležák
AMBER BEER 4.4% ABV
Brewed using caramalt for a nutty
bitterness, offset by toffee aromas
and a honeyed palate.

Big Sky

USA

5417 Trumpeter Way
Missoula, MT 59808,
www.bigskybrew.com

Three partners successfully combined
a quality ale with a clever name (albeit
one it had to defend in lawsuits lodged
by Canadian brewer Moosehead) and
an attractive label. Big Sky has grown
quickly into a regional brewery selling
beer from Alaska to Minnesota, three-
quarters of it their flagship brown ale.

Moose Drool
BROWN ALE 5.3% ABV
Dark fruits and nuts mingle with
chocolate; sweetness moderated by
earthy hop notes. Chocolate-brown
with a medium body.

Scape Goat Pale Ale
PALE ALE 4.7% ABV
Biscuity, fruity, and spicy on
the palate, balanced by moderate
bitterness. Short but dry finish.

Birrificio Italiano

ITALY

Via Castello 51,
22070 Lurago Marinon (CO),
www.birrificio.it

Agostino Arioli founded his renowned
brewpub in 1994 with his brother
Stefano and other friends. His pils
and bock soon became cult favorites.
He brews a large range of seasonal
beers such as a sparkling blackcurrant
lager and a cask-conditioned ale
spiced with cinnamon and ginger.
The restaurant serves great regional
food and has live music.

Scires
CHERRY ALE 7% ABV
Whole black Vignola cherries,
lactic bacteria, wild yeast, and
wood chips create this fantastic
sour beer.

Fleurette
FLAVORED LIGHT ALE 3.7% ABV
Made with barley, wheat, and rye,
and flavored with rose and violet
petals, elderberry juice, black
pepper, and citrus honey.

Bischoff

GERMANY

Wellerhof, 50321 Brühl,
www.bischoff-koelsch.de

This privately owned brewery was
established in farm buildings at the
beginning of the 1960s, in an area
of Brühl, near Cologne, that has
been inhabited since Roman times.

BREWING SECRET The brewery's
kölsch is a specialty of the Cologne
region and is traditionally served
in a tall, narrow glass.

Bischoff Kölsch
KÖLSCH 4.9% ABV
Clear golden color; fresh and
sweet, with light notes of hops.

Radler
BEER BLEND 2.5% ABV
Clear yellow in color, with
lemonade-citrus aromas. It is
sparkling and very refreshing.

Bischofshof

GERMANY

Heitzerstr. 2, 93049 Regensburg,
www.bischofshof.de

The Bischofshof brewery started life
attached to Regensburg Cathedral.
Records show that it was brewing in
1230 for the Bishop. At the beginning
of the 20th century, it moved to a new
location in order to expand. Nowadays,
Bischofshof beer is produced in one
of the most modern facilities in the
brewing industry.

Weissbier Hell
WHEAT BEER 5.1% ABV
An old Bavarian specialty: fresh,
clear, sparkling, and slightly
sweet—in a pleasant way.

Bischofshof Pils
PILSNER 5.1% ABV
Creamy foam and a light,
sparkling start. Good bitter
taste; light aromas of fine hops.

Bitburger

GERMANY

Römermauer. 3, 54634 Bitburg/ Eifel,
www.bitburger.de

Founded in 1817, Bitburger is a pilsner
specialist. It is well known through
international sponsorship of sporting
events, and is widely regarded as the
best brewery for pilsner on draft.

BREWING SECRET The company
always uses two-row summer
barley, and its testing brewery
is unique in Germany.

Premium Pils
PILSNER **4.8%** ABV
A clear, typical pilsner with a
light, bitter taste; smooth, but
very dry. On draft it is fresh
and elegant.

Bitburger Light
PILSNER **2.8%** ABV
The light sister of the premium.
Though only 2.8% ABV, it is
full-bodied, with a fresh cask taste.

57

Black Sheep

ENGLAND

Masham, North Yorkshire,
HG4 4EN
www.blacksheepbrewery.com

The Theakston family has brewed
in Masham, North Yorkshire, for six
generations, but a loss of independence
led to Paul Theakston stepping aside.
He then established Black Sheep in a
former maltings sitting high above the
Ure River. Since 1992, Black Sheep has
enjoyed continuous growth, physically
and in reputation, resulting in a £5m
doubling of capacity in 2006.

Black Sheep Ale
BITTER 4.4% ABV
Full-flavored, with a rich,
fruity aroma, bitter-sweet
malty taste, and long, dry finish.

Riggwelter
PREMIUM BITTER 5.9% ABV
A strong, complex, fruity bitter,
with dashes of pear drops and
hints of liquorice.

Blaugies

BELGIUM

435, Rue de la Frontière,
B7370 Dour-Blaugies,
www.brasseriedeblaugies.com

Hard by the French border, Blaugies
is another small family brewery in
which the children have taken over from
the parents—who, in this case, started
up the business in 1988. The aim of
De Blaugies is to produce beers in the
style of the region, and the brewery
often creates highly unusual brews.

La Moneuse
SAISON 8% ABV
Down-to-earth, spicy Hainaut
brew: yeasty, estery; strong for
a *saison*, with the characteristic
metallic tang.

Bière Darbyste
FLAVORED ALE 5.4% ABV
Fig's juice? Alcoholic variant
of Yesteryear, a non-alcoholic
brew. Sweet only when fresh.

J Boag & Son

AUSTRALIA

39 William Street, Launceston,
Tasmania 7250,
www.boags.com.au

From a once-moribund regional brewery,
Boag's has ridden a wave of popularity
since the launch of James Boag's
Premium Lager in 1994. Lagers
comprise the bulk of production,
but Boag's has rolled out some fine
limited-edition ales in recent years.
The brewery was acquired by the
Lion Nathan group in late 2007.

Wizard Smith's Ale
BITTER ALE 5% ABV
A solid malt backbone, with toffee
and spicy hop notes, is rounded
out by a significant bitterness.

Bockor

BELGIUM

Kwabrugstraat 5, B8510 Bellegem,
www.bockor.be

This brewery is probably best known
for its Jacobins (would-be lambics
that use spontaneous fermentation).
However, the brewery turns out a
whole range of other beers, not least
a traditional style oud bruin, created
by former head brewer Omer Vander
Ghinste. Bockor is currently
revamping the range of beers.

Bellegems Bruin
**MIXED FERMENTATION BEER 5.5%
ABV**
Oud bruin relies both on wild and
cultivated yeasts. The result: a beer
in which flavors of berries, wood,
and lactic sourness abound.

Bøgedal Bryghus

DENMARK

Høllundvej 9, DK-7100 Vejle,
www.boegedal.com

This farmhouse is the world's only
commercial brewery producing the
old Danish style of "Goodbeer," a
strong, rich beer dating back to before
the industrial age. The same recipe is
always followed, and yet no two beers
are alike, hence they are numbered
rather than named.

BREWING SECRET Bøgedal is
Scandinavia's only all-gravity
brewery.

Brew No. 127
DARK ALE 6.3% ABV
Smells of prunes and citrus.
Fills the palate and lingers on
with a faint smoky aftertaste.

Brew No. 121
PALE ALE 5.9% ABV
Light amber in color with compact
carbonation. Aromatic sweetness
reaveals notes of honey, citrus,
and fine wine.

Boon

BELGIUM

Fonteinstraat 65,
B1520 Lembeek,
www.boon.be

In 1975, when lambic-based beers and
lambic brewers were dying out, Frank
Boon took over the De Vits range.
Deemed crazy, he still proves his
detractors wrong, by constantly
growing and improving his business.

BREWING SECRET Most Boon
beers are deemed "oude," meaning
"in the old style" of unadulterated
lambics.

Geuze Boon Mariage Parfait
GUEUZE 8% ABV
"Perfect marriage," meaning the
lambics, of course, resulting in
the brewers' favorite dry gueuze.

Boon Oude Kriek
KRIEKEN 6.5% ABV
A fully unsweetened krieken (sour
cherry) lambic, which makes this
beer a delight for tongue and eyes.

63

Boon Rawd

THAILAND

999 Samsen Road, Bangkok,
10300 www.boonrawd.co.th

Boon Rawd was founded in 1933 by
Phraya Bhirom Bhakdi, who had
toured Germany and Denmark to
learn about brewing. The brewery
is still owned by the Bhirom-Bhakdi
family. The company operates three
breweries in Thailand.

Singha
LAGER 6% ABV
A full-bodied barley malt beer with
a strong hop character. Clean to
taste, it complements spicy food.

Singha Light
LAGER 3.5% ABV
Lacks the complexity and vitality
of its stronger stablemate. It is
pale yellow of hue and thin to taste.

Boscos

USA

Various locations in Tennessee
and Arkansas,
www.boscosbeer.com

Since 1992 this brewpub chain has
been a leader in promoting greater
knowledge of beer in the mid-south.
Its pubs feature English-inspired
cask-conditioned ales, with customers
invited to participate as cellermen.

BREWING SECRET Flaming
Stone's brewing process involves
red-hot chunks of granite being
plunged into the wort to
caramelize the sugars.

Flaming Stone Beer
STEINBEER 4.8% ABV
Brewed in the manner of German
stein beers. Caramel, toffee,
and nuts throughout. Smoky,
dry finish.

Hefeweizen
HEFEWEIZEN 4.8% ABV
Classic bubblegum and banana
nose; softer fruity (more banana)
and creamy flavors, with
underlying spices including
light clove notes.

Bosteels

BELGIUM

Kerkstraat 96,
B9255 Buggenhout,
www.bestbelgianspecialbeers.be

It is now the seventh generation of
the Bosteels family that owns and
runs this brewery. In recent times,
they have shown a flair for flowing
with fashion—not only in the beers,
but also with spectacular glassware.

BREWING SECRET Tripel
Karmeliet, one of the flagship
beers, uses three grains in the
mash: barley, wheat, and oats.

Tripel Karmeliet
ABBEY TRIPLE 8% ABV
Smoked and spicy nose announces
a malt-dominated brew with a
roasted character—unusual for
a pale beer.

Deus Brut Des Flandres
BELGIAN STRONG ALE 11.5% ABV
The Dom Perignon lookalike
bottle shows that this is aimed at
upmarket drinkers; dry and spritzy.

Boulder

USA

2880 Wilderness Place
Boulder, CO 80301,
www.boulderbeer.com

The first US microbrewery outside
of California, Boulder has been
something of a poster child for the
"movement" because its partners began
brewing in a goat shed and it relied
on the largesse of domestic giant Coors
to acquire ingredients. Boulder Beer
is available in much of the US, and
emphasizes its Colorado roots.

Planet Porter
PORTER 5.1% ABV
The brewery's original beer. Dark
fruit aromas and flavors. Subdued
roasted malts and bitterness.

Hazed & Infused
PALE ALE 4.85% ABV
As hazy as promised—hops in
suspension—supported by a bouquet
of citrus, flowers, and spices.

67

Bourganel

FRANCE

7 avenue Claude Expilly,
07600 Vals les Bains,
www.bieres-bourganel.com

In 1997 Christian Bourganel, a drinks
distributor in the Ardèche, decided to
develop a range of blonde artisan beers
flavored with regional produce.

BREWING SECRET Unusual
ingredients include chestnuts
(*marrons*), bilberries (*myrtilles*),
nougat from Montélimar and
Verveine du Velay liqueur,
which is flavored with verbena.

Bourganel au Nougat
FLAVORED LAGER 5% ABV
An amazing nougat bouquet
and, in the mouth, the flavor
of grilled almonds.

Bourganel aux Marrons
FLAVORED LAGER 5% ABV
An amber beer; elegant, very fruity
and refreshing, with a hint of
vanilla as well as chestnut.

Brains

WALES

Crawshay Street, Cardiff,
Glamorgan, CF10 1SP
www.sabrain.com

A major force in regional brewing,
Brains is tremendously proud of its
Welsh heritage. Ales are produced in
a traditional fashion at the company's
landmark Cardiff Brewery, to which it
was relocated in 2000 from the nearby
Old Brewery, where the famous "pint
of Brains" had been produced for more
than 100 years.

Brains SA Gold
BEST BITTER 4.2% ABV
Its spirit aroma blends gentle malt
and spiced hop with malt-rich and
fruit flavors.

Brains Bitter
BITTER 3.7% ABV
Rich amber color, with subtle
malt and crisp hop aromas. Well
balanced, with some bitterness.

69

Brakspear

ENGLAND

Witney, Oxfordshire,
OX28 4DP
www.brakspear.co.uk

The long-established Brakspear
Brewery closed its Henley operation
in 2002, but the production of its beers
was taken on by Wychwood Brewery.

BREWING SECRET Wychwood
uses Brakspear's original
equipment to brew these beers,
including the unique "double drop"
wooden fermenting vessels, and
its complex yeast strain.

Brakspear Bitter
BITTER 3.4% ABV
An initial malt and well-hopped
bitterness develops into a
bittersweet and fruity finish.

Brakspear Special
STRONG BITTER 4.3% ABV
Full-bodied, with a hint of
sweetness and dry hop bitterness
before finishing citrus-fruity.

Brahma

BRAZIL

Rua São Cristóvão, 1221,
São Cristóvão,
Rio de Janeiro,
www.brahma.com

The Portuguese brought beer to Brazil
at the beginning of the 19th century
but it was Swiss immigrant Joseph
Villager who first brewed Brahma in
1888. Named after the Hindu god,
Brahma has grown to be one of the
world's most drunk beers. The company
is now part of Anheuser-Busch InBev.

Brahma
LAGER 4.8% ABV
Low in bitterness and light to
drink, it has a subtle fruity
aroma and no aftertaste.

Antarctica
LAGER 4.9% ABV
Light in color, bitterness, and
aroma, it is an easy drinking beer.

71

Braugold

GERMANY

Schillerstr. 7, 99096 Erfurt,
www.braugold.de

The brewery was founded in 1822, and
acquired other breweries over time—up
until 1948, the point at which it was
nationalized by the GDR. After
Reunification in 1990, Braugold was
purchased by the Licher Privatbrauerei.

BREWING SECRET The brewers
follow recipes from the famous
Thüringer brewery.

Braugold Spezial
PILSNER 4.9% ABV
Has the typical golden color and
dryness of a pilsner; highly
aromatic with a balanced
bitterness of hops on the palate.

Braugold Bock
BOCK 6.5% ABV
Its balanced, bitter aroma and
strong flavor are typical of a bock.

Brewer's Art

USA

106 N. Charles Street
Baltimore, MD 21201,
www.thebrewersart.com

Housed in a grand 1902 townhouse
in the Mount Vernon area, The
Brewer's Art serves Belgian-inspired
house beers and an outstanding
selection of continental (primarily
Belgian) beers in a comfortable dining
atmosphere. It recently began brewing
and bottling some of its beer under
contract in Pennsylvania.

Green Peppercorn Tripel
TRIPLE 10% ABV
Effervescent and full of life. Fruity
and spicy, a bit of candy sweetness,
subdued pepper, and a dryish finish.

Resurrection
DOUBLE 7% ABV
Caramel, dark fruits on the palate,
and surprising citrus notes. The
yeast in the first batch "died" and
was "resurrected," hence the name.

BridgePort

USA

1313 Northwest Marshall Street
Portland, OR 97209,
www.bridgeportbrew.com

BridgePort Brewing holds the
trademark of Oregon's Oldest Craft
Brewery, and its India Pale Ale has
come to define the Northwest's beer
character. Despite several expansions,
it remains Portland-oriented.
It dedicates each release of Old
Knucklehead, its seasonal barley
wine, to a different local personality.

India Pale Ale

INDIA PALE ALE **5.5% ABV**
Citrussy from the outset. Solid
malt backbone, delicate fruits
(peaches and apples). Complex
hoppy finish.

Black Strap Stout

STOUT **6% ABV**
A rich blend of black strap
molasses, chocolate and coffee,
finishing with roasted bitterness.

74

Brinkhoff

GERMANY

Lütgendortmunder Hellweg 242,
44388 Dortmund,
www.brinkhoffs.de

From its humble origins in 1844 as
a small home brewery, Brinkhoff has
had more than 160 years of success,
to become a brand known far beyond
its hometown of Dortmund, one of the
beer capitals of the world. Brinkhoff's
No. 1 is a notable name for every lover
of the special pilsners from this region.

Brinkhoff's No. 1
PILSNER 5% ABV
Typical bitter aromas of a pilsner.
Smooth, slightly sparkling, with
a golden-yellow color.

Brinkhoff's Radler
BEER BLEND 2.5% ABV
Honey-colored, sparkling, and
pleasant with citrus aromas; very
refreshing and not too sweet.

OREGON, USA

The term "Beervana" is often used to describe Oregon's culture of craft beer. Beer touring opportunities abound, and it would be possible to spend weeks traveling and never drink the same beer twice. This three-day trail starts in the seaside town of Newport, which is home to the iconic Rogue Ales brewery. It continues the next day with scenic stops on the way to Portland, then concludes with a full day in the Rose City. For more information visit www.oregonbeer.org.

1 DAY 1: **NEWPORT AND ROGUE ALES**
Rogue Ales Public House is located on OSU Drive, right in the center of the working seaport of Newport. There are plenty of bed and breakfasts to choose from in this friendly town, including Rogue's "Bed and Beer" apartments, above the public house. The public house is also the place to book in for one of the brewery tours, which commence at 3pm daily. *2320 OSU Drive, Newport (www.rogueales.com)*

2 DAY 2: **PELICAN PUB & BREWERY**
The scenic 48-mile (77-km) drive from Newport to Pacific City easily occupies a morning, so you should arrive just in time for lunch at the Pelican Pub & Brewery. The brewery-restaurant is located on the shoreline of Pacific City, where there are outstanding views of the oft-photographed Haystack Rock and Cape Kiwanda. *33180 Cape Kiwanda Drive, Pacific City (www.pelicanbrewery.com)*

3 DAY 2: **GOLDEN VALLEY BREWERY & PUB**
The scenic route to McMinnville passes through the Willamette Valley, one of the nation's premier wine-growing regions. The Golden Valley Brewery & Pub offers ales, sometimes aged in wine barrels. *980 East 4th St., McMinnville*

4 DAY 3: **PORTLAND**
With more than three dozen breweries in the metropolitan region, it is little wonder residents of Portland like to say they live in "Beervana." Here are some you could visit on Day 3 of this trail.

Hair of the Dog
This tiny brewery uses equipment not originally designed for brewing. Visits by appointment. *4509 SE 23rd Avenue, Portland (www.hairofthedog.com)*

Widmer (see p342)
Visit the brewery's Gasthaus restaurant to sample the full line-up of beers—including the Alt intended to be the brewery flagship before its Hefeweizen became an American standard. The brewery offers tours on Fridays and Saturdays. *929 North Russell, Portland*

BridgePort (see p74)
Oregon's oldest surviving brewery helped turn the Pearl District into a hip locale. *1313 Northwest Marshall Street, Portland*

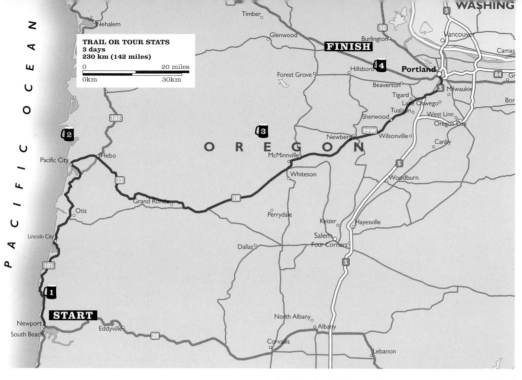

TRAIL OR TOUR STATS
3 days
230 km (142 miles)

0   20 miles
0km   30km

FINISH

START

Nehalem
Timber
Glenwood
Burlington
Vancouver
Camas
Forest Grove
Hillsboro
Portland
Beaverton
Tigard
Milwaukie
Lake Oswego
West Linn
Sherwood
Tualatin
Oregon City
Newberg
Wilsonville
Canby
McMinnville
Whiteson
Woodburn
Hebo
Pacific City
Otis
Grand Ronde
Perrydale
Keizer
Hayesville
Lincoln City
Salem
Four Corners
Dallas
Newport
South Beach
Eddyville
North Albany
Albany
Corvallis
Lebanon

Higgins Brewpub
Greg Higgins uses local produce for his widely praised menu, which pairs well with Oregon beers and wines.
1239 SW Broadway, Portland

Green Dragon Bistro and Pub
This relative newcomer quickly became an instant hit with a trendy crowd. Offers a constantly-changing selection of beers not necessarily found elsewhere, served by a knowledgeable staff.
928 SE 9th Avenue, Portland

Horse Brass Pub
A Portland institution since 1976, the Horse Brass is a sprawling tribute to both the English pub and Oregon beer, offering 52 selections on draft. The pub is especially popular with the late-night crowd.
4534 SE Belmont Street, Portland

Bristol

USA

1647 South Tejon
Colorado Springs, CO 80906,
www.bristolbrewing.com

Since opening in 1994, Bristol Brewing
has been the beer hub in Colorado
Springs, as others have come and gone.
It ventured into experimenting with
barrels ahead of many US breweries.

BREWING SECRET It has won
awards with a beer made using
wild yeast and lactic acid bacteria
from raspberries picked in nearby
Cheyenne Canyon.

Winter Warlock
OATMEAL STOUT 6.5% ABV
Toasted marshmallows and
chocolate up front, creamy
chocolate and roasted flavors
on the palate.

Laughing Lab
SCOTTISH ALE 5.3% ABV
Medium-bodied, with sweet
notes of caramel and toffee
and a lingering impression
of smoke. Best on tap.

Brøckhouse

DENMARK

Høgevej 6, DK-3400 Hillerød,
www.broeckhouse.dk

A fast-growing and popular
microbrewery to the north of
Copenhagen, established in 2002.
It was the goal of owner Allan
Poulsen, a former IT engineer,
to create something different
from ordinary Danish pilsner.

BREWING SECRET Poulsen uses
quality ingredients and British,
German, and Belgian brewing
traditions to create exciting and
memorable brews.

Brøckhouse IPA
INDIAN PALE ALE 6% ABV
Top-fermented ale brewed with
three varieties of hops to achieve
a sweet, balanced complexity.

Brøckhouse Esrum Kloster
ABBEY ALE 7.5% ABV
Developed with the monks of
Esrum Abbey. Strong nose; sweet,
spicy flavor with hints of aniseed,
lavender, rosemary, and juniper.

Brooklyn

USA

1 Brewers Row
79 North 11th Street
Brooklyn, NY 11211,
www.brooklynbrewery.com

While Brooklyn Brewery pays homage
to New York's rich brewing history, it is
very much a 21st-century business, and
occupies New York's first commercial
building to derive all of its electricity
from wind power. The brewery's bottled
beers are made under contract in upstate
New York, while brewmaster Garrett
Oliver regularly produces seasonals
and a reserve series at the brewery,
sold on tap throughout the region.

Brooklyner Weisse
HEFEWEIZEN 5.1% ABV
Effervescent and banana-fruity
from the start, backed up with
spices, hops, and gentle clove notes.

Local 1
BELGIAN STRONG GOLDEN ALE 9% ABV
An explosion of aromas and flavors
of fruits and spices, and a complex
texture, all brought together with
a chalky-dry finish.

Brouwerij 't IJ

NETHERLANDS

Funenkade 7,
1018 AL Amsterdam,
www.brouwerijhetij.nl

Amsterdam's favorite micro is now
the city's oldest brewery, even though
it was founded only in 1985. Strong
Belgian-style ales form the backbone
of the output, though there's also a pils
and a witbier. Set in an old windmill,
the taproom is thronged on warm
summer afternoons, its outdoor seating
taken up by drinkers enjoying the
lowest beer prices in Amsterdam.

Turbock
DOPPELBOCK 9% ABV
Packed with dark fruits and
molasses sweetness, the trademark
IJ spiciness adds a dimension not
found in German bocks.

Columbus
STRONG ALE 9% ABV
A balance of biscuity malt,
coriander, lemon, and resinous,
minty hops. Assertive, but not
overpowering.

81

B

BrowArmia

POLAND

Ul. Królewska 1,
Warszawa, 00-065,
www.browarmia.pl

Opened in 2005, this fine brewpub has a
vibrant atmosphere—busy, convivial, and
loud on music nights. Polish food with a
modern twist is a specialty to match the
beers on tap. Six beers are currently
brewed in the smart cellar brewery,
with six more planned for the future.

Pszenciczne
PALE ALE 4.8% ABV
Not quite a Burton ale, it is
strongly hopped in the kettle
before being dry-hopped in
the lagering tank.

Raspberry Wheat Beer
WHEAT BEER 5% ABV
The house wheat beer is in the
Bavarian style, with the addition
of fresh raspberries. The fruit
adds a refreshing, zesty tartness.

Bucher Bräu

GERMANY

Elsenthaler Str. 5-7,
9441 Grafenau,
www.bucher-braeu.de

A medium-sized brewery that moved
to the heart of the Bavarian Forest in
1982 after outgrowing its premises
in the center of Grafenau. It has been
owned by the Bucher family since
1863 (now in its fifth generation).

BREWING SECRET The natural
cloudiness of the Hefeweizen
comes from the yeast added
at the time of bottling.

Grafenauer Hefeweizen
WHEAT BEER 5.2% ABV
Fresh and sparkling. The light
taste of yeast is fine and aromatic.
There is a little sweetness.

Helles
LAGER 4.9% ABV
Clear yellow beer, slightly bitter,
with a reasonable sweetness, and
a taste of the finest hops. A rather
strong but rounded finish.

83

Budels

NETHERLANDS

Nieuwstraat 9,
6020 AA Budel,
www.budels.nl

Budels is among the few established,
predominantly bottom-fermenting
Dutch breweries. Started in 1870, the
business is currently run by the fourth
generation of the founding Aerts family.

BREWING SECRET In recent
years Budels has diversified into
top-fermenting beers, such as kölsch,
altbier, and an abbey-style dubbel.

Budels Lager
PILS 5% ABV
A gentle, piney hop aroma is followed
by fruity, sweetish taste; perhaps
closer to a helles than a pils.

Budels Capucijn
ABBEY-STYLE DOUBLE 6.5% ABV
Sweet toasted malt aromas are
complemented by bitterness, dates,
and the merest hint of smoke.

84

Budweiser Budvar

CZECH REPUBLIC

Karolíny Světle 4, 370 21
České Budějovice,
www.original-budweiser.cz

The town of České Budějovice (Budweis) has been a home of brewing since 1265. Today, the Budějovický (Budweiser) Budvar product name has Protected Geographical Indicator status within the EU (like Cognac and Parma ham), but in the US, where Anheuser-Busch's Budweiser is trademarked, it is called Czechvar.

Budweiser Budvar / Czechvar
PREMIUM LAGER 5% ABV
Spritzy, with an attractive head, floral and grapefruit fruitiness on the nose, and a dry, biscuit malt palate.

Czech Dark Lager
DARK BEER 4.7% ABV
Its distinct malty flavor develops a cinnamon spiciness before rolling into biscuit undertones.

Caldera

USA

540 Clover Lane
Ashland, OR 97520,
www.calderabrewing.com

Although it's been around since 1997, Caldera has enjoyed increased visibility and distribution since 2005, when it became the first microbrewery in Oregon to install a small-run line for its distinctively packaged canned beers.

BREWING SECRET Caldera sets itself apart by continuing to use whole hop flowers in all its beers.

IPA

INDIA PALE ALE 6.7% ABV
Makes a large hop impression without being heavy-handed. Citrus, pine, and grapefruit from start to finish.

Pilsener

PILSNER 5% ABV
Gets eight full weeks of lagering. Floral aroma, with just an initial hint of sulfur, with a crisp, hoppy flavor and finish.

Caledonian

SCOTLAND

42 Slateford Road,
Edinburgh, EH11 1PH
www.caledonian-brewery.co.uk

The Caledonian attitude to brewing
beer is similar to that of drinking
it—the longer you've been doing it, the
more quality you demand. It is the sole
survivor of some 40 breweries that
once resided in Edinburgh.

BREWING SECRET Caledonian
is one of the last breweries to use
traditional direct-fired coppers
to boil the wort.

Caledonian 80 Shilling
SCOTTISH HEAVY 4.2% ABV
Russett-brown and typically
malt-led, with an underlay
of raspberry and a suggestion
of chocolate.

Deuchars IPA
INDIA PALE ALE 3.8% ABV
A strident hop aroma, with citrus
notes and a degree of maltiness
that never wavers.

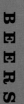

GREAT **C** BEERS

Cantillon

BELGIUM

Gheudestraat 56,
B1070 Brussel/Anderlecht,
www.cantillon.be

As early as 1900, the Cantillon family had beer blending facilities here, in the old southern suburbs of Brussels. In 1970, Jean-Pierre Van Roy, who had married Claude Cantillon, took over the business, becoming a staunch defender of old-style brewing. His son Jean, however, has shown in the last 10 years or so that the brewery is not averse to experimentation, on occasion using fresh hops, and even American "C-hops"—both anathema to the lambic tradition.

Cantillon Gueuze
ORGANIC LAMBIC 5% ABV
Nose of citrus, horse blanket, wood, and hay; woody flavors, with green fruit and some sulfur; sour and tart in mouthfeel.

Lou Pepe Framboise
FRUIT BEER 5.5% ABV
A mix of lambic beer with a pure sugar solution. One of the most intense fruit beers on earth.

GREAT C BEERS

Capital

USA

7734 Terrace Avenue
Middleton, WI 53562,
www.capital-brewery.com

Capital Brewery is known for its
excellent German-inspired beers—
brewed in copper kettles from a defunct
German brewery—though some are
made with a twist. Autumnal Fire,
for instance, is a cross between a
doppelbock and an Oktoberfest-style ale.

BREWING SECRET The grain
for Capital's Island Wheat is grown
on an island in Lake Michigan.

Munich Dark
DARK LAGER 5.4% ABV
Malt-accented, with early hints
of caramel and nuts. Building
richness with chocolate-toffee
notes.

Special Pilsner
PILSNER 4.8% ABV
Light on the palate with a note of
honey. Lovely floral hop aromas
and a sturdy hop finish.

Captain Lawrence

USA

99 Castleton Street
Pleasantville, NY 10570,
www.captainlawrencebrewing.com

Brewmaster-owner Scott Vaccaro represents the newest generation of American brewers, with a formal education in brewing science, then on-the-job training in the US and England. Back in his home state, he founded this brewery with the support of his family. He is at the forefront in experimention with barrel ageing.

Xtra Gold
TRIPLE 9% ABV
Citrus notes from Northwest hops blend seamlessly with juicy orchard fruits and a bit of candy sweetness.

Smoked Porter
PORTER 6.4% ABV
Smoky to start, but rich dark fruits, chocolate, and liquorice quickly emerge. Luscious palate.

Caracole

BELGIUM

86, Côte Marie-Thérèse,
B5500 Falmignoul,
www.brasserie-caracole.be

Started in around 1990, Caracole moved
after a few years from Namur to the
present location. The brewery offers
beers in two varieties: a "normal," and
a "bio" (organic) version. Caracole
means "snail," and production isn't
rushed—but the beers are enjoying
growing international recognition.

Troublette Bio
WITBIER 5% ABV
A fully organic Belgian white,
with no excess coriander, but a
fine citrussy and refreshing finish.

Nostradamus
BELGIAN DARK ALE 9.5% ABV
Caracole's strong dark ale is
a mix of roasted, fruity, malty,
and higher alcohol notes.

91

Carib

TRINIDAD

Eastern Main Road,
Champs Fleurs,
www.caribbeer.com

The sole brewery on Trinidad since
1957, Carib has formed business links
with InBev, Carlsberg, and Diageo—the
owner of Guinness. The company also
has breweries in Grenada, St. Kitts,
and Nevis. The British brought
commercial brewing to Trinidad just
after World War I; the local taste favors
sweet lagers and strong stouts.

Carib Lager
LAGER 5.2% ABV
Pale, but full-bodied with a rich
head formation. Slightly aromatic,
balanced between sweet and bitter.

Carib Stag
LAGER 5.9% ABV
European style lager. It is has a
pale golden straw color with a rich
head formation. Very sweet.

Cascade

AUSTRALIA

131 Cascade Road,
South Hobart,
Tasmania 7004,
www.cascadebrewery.com.au

Australia's oldest operating brewery,
complete with on-site maltings, is also
the most striking, with the castellated
sandstone building nestled in the
foothills of the sometimes snow-capped
Mount Wellington. Now part of the
Foster's empire, Cascade attracts
tens of thousands of beer lovers
annually to its visitor center.

Cascade Stout
MEDIUM STOUT 5.8% ABV
Coffee notes up front, with milk
chocolate on the palate, followed
by a moderately bitter finish.

Cascade Blonde
SUMMER ALE 4.8% ABV
Clean and crisp, with
a hint of citrus hop flavor.

GREAT **C** BEERS

93

Castelain

FRANCE

13 rue Pasteur,
62410 Bénifontaine,
www.chti.com

Founded in 1926, this family brewery
was passed into the hands of Yves
and Annick Castelain from their
parents in 1978. Under the name of
Ch'ti (local patois for a northerner),
they have developed a range of strong,
mellow lager beers with a long, cold
secondary fermentation period.

Maltesse
PREMIUM LAGER 7.7% ABV
Blonde, rich, and strong, with a
taste of barley, and an appealing
hint of bitterness in the finish.

Ch'ti Blonde
LAGER 6.4% ABV
Full-bodied, with just enough
bitterness to be very refreshing.
Mellow and tasty.

94

Castle / SAB

SOUTH AFRICA

65 Park Lane,
Sandown,
Sandtona,
www.sablimited.co.za

SAB—South African Breweries—was founded in 1895 and began producing its Castle Lager brand in the mining town of Johannesburg. The company soon became the biggest brewer in southern Africa. In 2002, SAB bought Miller Brewing in the US, and as SABMiller it has become one of the biggest global drinks companies.

Castle Lager
LAGER 5% ABV
Award-winning lager made from African Gold Barley and Southern Star hops. It is brewed in nine countries and sold in 40.

Castle Milk Stout
MILK STOUT 6% ABV
Dark, highly-hopped, strong stout with a complex taste of roasted black malts, coffee, and caramel.

C

Cēsu Alus

LATVIA

Aldaru laukums 1,
Cēsis, 4101
www.cesualus.lv

Cēsu Alus was founded in 1879 and is
the oldest brewery in Latvia. In 1999 it
was purchased by the Estonian brewer
A. Le Coq. It is now one of the largest
brewers in Latvia. It has a new, state-of-
the-art brewhouse and further huge
investment is being planned. The
town is renowned for its beer festival,
knights' tournaments, and open-air
theater performances.

Cēsu Premium
LAGER 5.2% ABV
Sweet chocolate taste with hints of
aromatic vanilla. In Latvia, balsam
is commonly used to flavor drinks.

Cēsu Balsam Porter
PORTER 6% ABV
A pale golden color, it has hints of
sweet grass and hops on the nose.

Chimay

BELGIUM

8, Route Charlemagne,
B6464 Baileux,
www.chimay.com

Though the bottling is done in Baileux,
the brewery is still in the monastery at
Forges-les-Chimay. Since 1861, monks
have brewed here, but Chimay became
the leading Trappist brewery through
Père Theodore, who went to Leuven
University to study brewing in a
contemporary way. Chimay never
stopped growing and is vital to the
economy of the region.

Chimay Tripel
ABBEY ALE 8% ABV
Sweet, grapey taste, with bittering
hops and herbal qualities; not
entirely unlike a dry white wine.

Grande Réserve / Bleue
BELGIAN STRONG ALE 9% ABV
Roasted malts, with some quite
dominant bitterness, and dark,
ripe fruit (plums, blue grapes),
and pears.

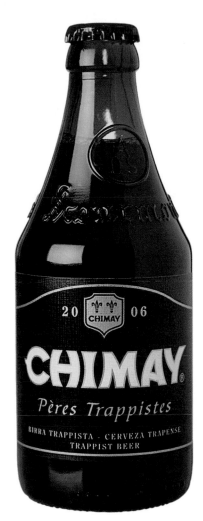

La Choulette

FRANCE

18 rue des Écoles,
59111 Hordain,
www.lachoulette.com

Founded in 1885, this farmhouse
brewery is a rare survivor from the
thousands of breweries that existed
in the region in the late 19th century.
Alain Dhaussy, the current brewer,
has succeeded in creating artisan beers
of real quality, faithful to the traditions
of northern France, but with a real
sense of innovation too.

Choulette Framboise
FRUIT BEER 6% ABV
Refreshing, with a slight sourness.
The note of ripe raspberries is
present, but not too intrusive.

Porte Du Hainaut Ambrée
AMBER ALE 7% ABV
Medium-bodied fruity beer, with
flavors of cooked apples, pears,
and caramel; slight bitterness.

Coopers

AUSTRALIA

461 South Road, Regency Park,
delaide, South Australia 5010,
www.coopersbrewery.com.au

While most Australian breweries were
progressively "lagerized" during the
20th century, this family-run Adelaide
brewing dynasty kept knocking out
cloudy, bottle-conditioned ales and
stouts. Since opening a new expanded
brewery in 2001, surging demand for
their beers has driven them to become
the country's third-largest beermaker.

Coopers Sparkling Ale
AUSTRALIAN PALE ALE 5.8% ABV
Cloudy; fruity aromatics with
a hint of peaches; rounded,
dry, yeasty finish.

Coopers Extra Stout
DRY STOUT 6.4% ABV
Espresso and bitter chocolate
notes, with banana hints too;
robustly bitter finish.

Coors

USA

311 10th Street
Golden, CO 80401,
www.coors.com

Although it merged with Molson, and that company now partners SABMiller in the US, Coors has continued to develop less mainstream beers. Its Blue Moon line competes with the largest craft brands, and its SandLot Brewery, within the Coors Field baseball stadium in Denver, regularly offers outstanding traditional lagers.

Blue Moon Belgian White
WITBIER 5.4% ABV
Citrussy sweet nose, spicy with notes of celery. Some wheat sourness, finishing on the sweet side.

Barmen Pilsner
PILSNER 5% ABV
Beautiful billowing head when poured correctly. Rich with Saaz hops, floral and spicy. Pleasantly grainy, with a long, bitter finish.

Cornelyshaff

LUXEMBOURG

Maison 37,9753 Heinerscheid,
www.cornelyshaff.lu

Situated in a nature park, Cornelyshaff
comprises a popular bar, restaurant,
and hotel, as well as a brewery that is
open to visitors. It is modern, gleaming,
and energy efficient—the cooperative
that owns it prides itself on minimizing
its environmental impact. The bar and
restaurant showcase the beers and
much farm produce from the area.

Ourdaller Waïssen Tarwebier
WITBIER 4.6% ABV
An unfiltered, cloudy wheat beer;
assertive in character, it is full of spice.

Kornelysbéier
RYE BEER 4.2% ABV
A spicy aroma gives way to a strongly
flavored deep, earthy taste brought on
by the use of rye grain.

Crailsheimer Engelbräu

GERMANY

Haller Str. 29,
74564 Crailsheim,
www.engelbier.de

When this brewery was founded by Georg Fach
in 1738, Crailsheim had 4,000 inhabitants and
13 breweries. Fach was not to know that his
company would become one of the most
successful in the country.

BREWING SECRET A survey
of what women like in a beer
led to the creation of the First
Lady brand.

First Lady
DUNKLER BOCK 5.9% ABV
Mild, lightly bitter, and with
a harmonious malty aroma.

Kellerbier Dunkel
DUNKEL 5.3% ABV
Beautiful mahogany color; aromas
of malt and yeast; full-bodied,
with a taste that is both sweet
and pleasantly bitter.

Creemore Springs

CANADA

Ontario, L0M 1G0,
www.creemoresprings.com

Ownership by Molsons since 2005 has
done little to lessen the independence
of this 100-year-old brewery. The town
of Creemore nestles between the
curiously named Mad and Noisy
rivers. Every August the brewery
is a sponsor of a town-center party
called the Copper Kettle Festival.
Regular brewery tours are run.

Premium Lager
LAGER 5% ABV
Soft malt and fruit flavors
give way to nutty overtones
and a dry hoppy finish.

Urbock
BOCK 6% ABV
Dark brown, with a sweet, nutty
texture; fruit aromas can be found
as the beer warms in the glass.

Darmstädter

GERMANY

Goebelstr. 7,
64293 Darmstadt,
www.darmstaedter.de

The brewery stands next to the train station in Darmstadt—hence the train logo, used since 1847, and the animated steam engine on its website.

BREWING SECRET A revolution in the company's history was the complete change-over of all bottles to clip-tops in the year 2000.

Pilsner
PILSNER 4.8% ABV
A clear and elegant beer. A large amount of fine hops make this a typical pilsner: fresh and dry with a good bitter aroma.

1847 Zwickelbier
LAGER 4.8% ABV
Unfiltered and cloudy with subtle aromas of fine malt and a smooth, yeasty taste.

104

Darwin

ENGLAND

Sunderland,
Tyne & Wear, SR1 2QE
www.darwinbrewery.com

The Darwin set-up is unique in that its commercial operation is complemented by a test brew plant based at the University of Sunderland. There, students on the Brewlab brewing sciences course are able to trial some 40 new beers each year. The best of them are then produced at the award-winning site.

Evolution Ale
BITTER **4% ABV**
Light, clean, and satisfying, with a dry, hoppy character and layers of malt throughout.

Ghost Ale
BITTER **4.1% ABV**
Golden and richly hopped, with citrus aromas dominating, followed by a well-balanced fruit piquancy.

Deschutes

USA

901 Southwest Simpson Avenue, Bend,
OR 97702,
www.deschutesbrewery.com

What began with a brewpub in 1988 quickly expanded with a separate production facility that's grown into one of the nation's largest craft breweries. As well as selling a full line of beers with notable hop character throughout the western US, Deschutes still operates its original brewpub in downtown Bend and another in Portland. A Bond Street Series of special beer releases, developed "at the pub," has further widened the brewery's portfolio.

Mirror Pond
PALE ALE 5.2% ABV
Grapefruit and fresh flowers at the outset. Light, clean biscuit on the palate, with generous hop flavor.

Inversion IPA
INDIA PALE ALE 6.8% ABV
A swirl of hop aromas (particularly orange zest). Solid, biscuity malt holds its own against bracing bitterness.

Desnoes and Geddes

JAMAICA

214 Spanish Town, Kingston,
www.jamaicadrinks.com

Now owned by global drinks giant
Diageo, Desnoes and Geddes was
established by two friends, Eugene
Desnoes and Thomas Geddes, who set
up a soft drink plant in 1918 and
began brewing in 1927 with Red Stripe.

BREWING SECRET Red Stripe
was originally produced as an
English ale. It didn't become
popular until it was offered
as a chilled lager instead.

Dragon Stout
SWEET STOUT 7.5% ABV
Having been primed with sugar
on bottling, the flavor is malty,
with a distinct note of molasses.

Dragon Gold
LAGER 5.5% ABV
Yellow in color, it has a grainy
aroma, a crisp, clean taste,
and is best drunk very cold.

107

Dětenice

CZECH REPUBLIC

Pivovar Dětenice, 507 24 Dětenice,
www.krcmadetenice.cz

The castle-based brewery—once owned
by the Prague chapter of the Knights
of Malta—closed in 1955 after several
years of nationalization, and reopened
only in 2000.

BREWING SECRET Beers are
brewed in direct-fired vessels
and are filtered through straw,
fermented in wooden vats,
then lagered in oak barrels.

Svetlé Detenické Pivo 12°
PREMIUM LAGER 4% ABV
Aromatically floral, finely
structured body; sweet malt
and honey influences, and
hoppy afterglow.

Tmavé Detenicke Pivo 13°
DARK BEER 4% ABV
A typically full-bodied dark lager;
malty, some spice, and faintly
bitter toward the finish.

D

Diebels

GERMANY

Brauerei-Diebels-Str. 1,
47661 Issum,
www.diebels.de

Diebels was privately owned from 1878 until 2001, when the brewery was taken over by global drinks giant InBev. The Düsseldorfer Alt is the brewery's most famous brand and is sold all over Germany. Other, newer brands include a pilsner and a cola-blended beer called Dimix.

Diebels Alt
ALTBIER 4.9% ABV
Roasted malt aromas harmonize with a sweet caramel taste; the finish is slightly bitter from hops.

Diebels Pils
PILSNER 4.9% ABV
The full-body, light bitterness, and malt aromas are typical of a pilsner, as is the dark golden color.

D

Dinkelacker-Schwabenbräu

GERMANY

Tübinger Str. 46, 70178 Stuttgart,
www.ds-kg.de

Carl Dinkelacker was the first to brew
pilsner in Stuttgart at the end of the
19th century, and his contemporary
Robert Leicht was the first to deliver
beer by car. Today, their breweries are
in partnership and together form the
biggest player in Baden-Württemberg.

Dinkelacker Privat
LAGER **5.1%** ABV
A fine, smooth, and clear golden
lager with a mild aroma of hops
and a light note of malt.

Dinkelacker CD-Pils
PILSNER **4.9%** ABV
Noble dry pilsner with strong
aromas of hops and light malts;
very harmonious and pleasant.

Distelhäuser

GERMANY

Grünsfelder Str. 3, 97941
Tauberbischofsheim,
www.distelhaeuser.de

The Bauer family has owned this
brewery since 1876. It is situated on
the famous "Romantic Street" in
Tauberbischofsheim, which is closely
associated with the German Romantic
period. The long-standing success of
the brewery is due to its attention to
quality over the course of its history.

Distelhäuser Landbier
EXPORT 5.1% ABV
Malty aroma and a slightly
caramel taste; it has a mild
sweetness and is rounded
at the finish. Sometimes
described as a "ladies' beer."

Distelhäuser Pils
PILSNER 4.9% ABV
Topped by a snow-white foam, this
beer has a harmonious bitterness
and a great aroma of hops.

Dithmarscher

GERMANY

Oesterstr. 18,
25709 Marne Holstein,
www.dithmarscher.de

This brewery, on the east coast of
Schleswig-Holstein, has been operating
for more than 230 years. It started as a
small home brewery; today it is bigger,
but the beers are still handmade.

BREWING SECRET The sparkle
comes from using the charmant
method of pressurized
fermentation, and the addition
of dry, fresh carbonic acid.

Dithmarscher Dunkel
DUNKEL 4.9% ABV
This beer has a full-bodied
charmant character and a spicy
taste with notes of roastiness.
A typical color: dark mahogany.

Dithmarscher Pils
PILSNER 4.8% ABV
A mild and spicy beer, golden-
yellow in color, slightly sparkling.

Dixie

USA

2401 Tulane Avenue
New Orleans, LA 70119,
www.distinguished-brands.com/dixie.php

The 100-year-old Dixie Brewery was
the last survivor of New Orleans'
once-flourishing brewing tradition,
with some of its beers aged in
historic cypress barrels. That is,
until Hurricane Katrina (and the
subsequent looters) devastated it
in 2005. It's not clear when it might
reopen. Meanwhile its beers are
being made at the Minhaus Craft
Brewery in Wisconsin.

Blackened Voodoo
SCHWARZBIER 5% ABV
In 1991, this dark lager was
briefly banned in Texas because
of the voodoo references on its
label. Smooth and light-bodied for
southern drinking, with chocolate
and toffee notes throughout.

113

Döbler

GERMANY

Kornmarkt 6,
91438 Bad Windsheim,
www.brauhaus-doebler.de

Döbler celebrated its 140th anniversary in 2007. Production was traditional until 1950, after which the brewery switched to creating young-styled beers using technologically advanced equipment.

BREWING SECRET The barley has come from sustainable sources since 1986.

Land Märzen
MÄRZEN 5.4% ABV
A very light märzen; dark yellow, with a pleasant taste, not too sweet, but full-bodied with a nice yeast finish.

Reichsstadtbier
KELLERBIER 5% ABV
Full-bodied, unfiltered, and cloudy, with a taste of yeast. It is available on draft.

Dogfish Head

USA

6 Cannery Village Center
Milton, DE 19968,
www.dogfish.com

Dogfish Head has found a national
audience for its "extreme beers." These
have included ales developed using
research from archaeologists; recipes
featuring unusual ingredients, from
chicory to chilies; and beers that simply
have more of everything. The brewery
recently installed the largest wooden
brewing vessels built in the US since
before Prohibition. Dogfish still operates
a brewpub in Rehoboth Beach, where
founder Sam Calagione started in 1995.

Midas Touch
HISTORIC BEER 9% ABV
The ingredients—white Muscat
grapes, honey, and saffron—create
layers of flavor, melded with subtle
acidity.

60 Minute IPA
INDIA PALE ALE 6% ABV
Flagship session beer brewed with
Warrior, Amarillo, and "Mystery Hop
X," and brimming with citrus flavors.

De Dolle Brouwers

BELGIUM

oeselarestraat 12B,
B8600 Esen,
www.dedollebrouwers.be

By buying and renewing the old
Costenoble Brewery in 1980, Kris
Herteleer and his two brothers started,
unknowingly, Belgium's microbrewery
revolution. Fame soon reached
international quarters—but then
the "mad brewers" never searched
for simplicity, a quiet life, or easy
money. "Quality does the trick" is
the motto of Kris—the only remaining
brewer of the original three.

Oerbier
BELGIAN DARK ALE 9% ABV
Fruitiness throughout, from
nose to finish. Very vinous
character, grapey, and
clearly strong in alcohol.

Arabier
SEASONAL CHRISTMAS ALE 12% ABV
Overripe grapes, raisins, and other
dried fruits. Some hoppy bitterness
hiding behind lots of sweet malts;
acidic lining for a great balance.

Double Maxim

ENGLAND

Hughton-le-Spring,
Sunderland,
www.dmbc.org.uk

After several years contracting out
the company's eponymous beer, a new
brewery was opened in 2007 to cope
with demand. Bottling facilities are
planned for the near future.

BREWING SECRET Double
Maxim uses an original Vaux
Brewery recipe, which head brewer
Jim Murray used when he worked
at Vaux in 1968.

Double Maxim
BROWN ALE 4.7% ABV
Caramel in the aroma; continues
through bittersweet flavors, then
expands into toffee notes.

Samson
BEST BITTER 4.6% ABV
A dependable northeast English
bitter, with a whiff of hop and a
malt-infused body.

117

D

Dreher

HUNGARY

Magladi ut 17, Budapest,
www.dreher.hu

For many years this brewery was run
by Anton Dreher, one of the great beer
innovators. In the mid-19th century,
he developed the technology to ferment
beer at low temperatures and created
a new kind of malty amber beer, called
Vienna lager. For his achievements,
Dreher was dubbed "The King of Beer."
The company is now owned by SABMiller.

Dreher Classic
PILSNER 5.5% ABV
With a crisp, fresh aroma, this is
a bitter, golden-yellow beer with
an aroma of hops and a hint of malt.

Dreher Bak
DUNKLER BOCK 7.3% ABV
A rich, full-bodied dark beer, notes
of caramel and malt, reminiscent
of bittersweet chocolate.

Dubuisson

BELGIUM

28, Chaussée de Mons,
B7904 Pipaix-Leuze,
www.br-dubuisson.com

Leuze is a town with three breweries, two
of them in the Pipaix village. Dubuisson
is probably the most dynamic, and its
location, next to a major road, has made
their brewery tap a very successful
venture. The brewery excels in high
alcohol ales, so extreme caution is
advised when drinking these beers.

Bush Prestige
BELGIAN STRONG ALE 13% ABV
This oak-aged version of
the Ambrée is a true marvel
in balance, despite its
impressive strength.

Bush Ambrée
BELGIAN STRONG ALE 12% ABV
In some markets known as
"Scaldis," this is a treacherously
drinkable alcohol-bomb.

Ducato

ITALY

Via Strepponi 50/A,
43010 Roncole Verdi di Busseto (PR),
www.birrificiodelducato.it

Young brewer Giovanni Campari set
up his microbrewery in 2007 near
Giuseppe Verdi's birthplace, not far
from Parma. He proved his skills
from the outset, brewing four beers
full of character. Further new lines
are confirming Ducato as one of the
most promising Italian craft breweries.

New Morning
SAISON 5.6% ABV
Amazing saison, flavored with
camomile flowers. Easy-drinking
and thirst-quenching, with lovely
earthy notes.

AFO
AMERICAN PALE ALE 5.2% ABV
AFO means "Ale For the Obsessed"
and is dedicated to hop lovers. Nice
citrus fruit aromas, caramel notes.

Duck-Rabbit

USA

4519 W Pine Street
Farmville, NC 27828,
www.duckrabbitbrewery.com

Known for darkly intense beers, this
is one of several small breweries that
have thrived since North Carolina
changed its law to allow beer stronger
than 6% ABV. Duck-Rabbit's distinctive
logo is based on an illustration by
philosopher Ludwig Wittgenstein.

BREWING SECRET These
quirky brewers say "We sing
softly to the yeast."

Baltic Porter
BALTIC PORTER 9% ABV
Caramel, toffee, blackcurrants,
and other dark fruits, perfectly
blended. Smooth, with restrained
bitterness.

Milk Stout
STOUT 5.7% ABV
A well-integrated combination of
roasted coffee beans and chocolate,
held together by a creamy palate.
Sweet, but not too sweet.

121

Dugges Ale & Porterbryggeri

SWEDEN

Möbelgatan 3, SE-43133 Mölndal,
www.dugges.se

The brewery was founded in 2005 by
Mikael Dugge Engström. His series
of beers include Gothenburg, marrying
old Swedish traditions with British and
American inspiration, and Express
Yourself, a collection of specialty brews
with names like Holy Cow (an IPA) and
Fuggedaboudit! (a brown ale).

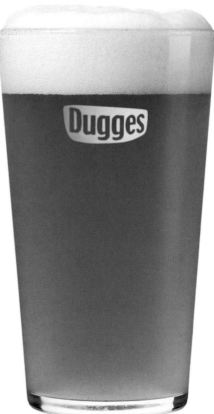

Dugges Avenyn Ale
AMERICAN PALE ALE 5% ABV
Aromas of hops, flowers, and
citrus fruits; flavors of grapes,
pine, and a hint of caramel.

High Five!
INDIAN PALE ALE 7.5% ABV
Dark amber. Intense hop aroma;
notes of strawberry jam, pine, and
chocolate, and a dry bitterness.

Dupont

BELGIUM

Brasserie Dupont, 5 Rue Basse,
B7904 Tourpes-Leuze,
www.brasserie-dupont.com

Western-Hainaut enjoys rich soil, and
farmsteads here were huge—usually
operating a brewery in the winter, making
beer to be consumed on the land in summer
(hence the style of beer known as saison).
Brasserie Dupont became solely a brewery,
but owner Olivier Dedeycker has re-
engaged with the history of the land,
by reintroducing farming and cheese-
making into this marvellous brewery.

Avec Les Bons Vœux
SEASONAL WINTER ALE 9.5% ABV
Once a complimentary winter ale,
but so superb that it is now brewed
year round. Barnyard and earthy
aromas mingle with citrus zest.
Grainy flavor: fresh white bread
with nuts, spices, and walnut oil.

Saison Dupont
SAISON 6.5% ABV
Formerly brewed in winter with
the hot summer months in mind—
hence a dry, refreshingly light brew.

123

BEER TRAIL

BRUSSELS, BELGIUM

"B" is for Belgium, Brussels, and Beer. Today, Belgian beers can be drunk worldwide, but the very best place to embrace Belgian beer culture is in Brussels itself, with its unique cafés, bars, and brasseries.

1 TOONE
The Beer Temple (*Rue Marché Aux Herbes 56*) is one of the world's best beer shops. It stocks most of Belgium's artisanal brewers. It is close to a narrow alleyway that forms the entrance to Toone, a puppet theater with a bar. The walls of this hidden gem are adorned with staring marionettes and the atmosphere is as good as the Kwak beer served here—in the correct glass of course.
6 Impasse Schuddevelde, off 21 Petit Ruedes Bouchers, Brussels

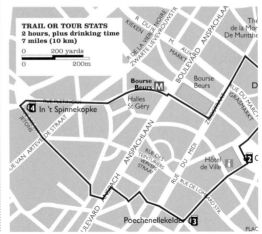

2 GRAND PLACE
Brussels' famous Grand Place is home to the Belgian Brewers Association and Brewery Museum—both occupy the opulent Brewers House. Several bars surround the square, but there are even better places to drink nearby. In September the square hosts an annual beer festival.

3 POECHENELLEKELDER
Opposite one of the world's most improbable tourist attractions, the Manneken Pis, is the Poechenellekelder. Loved by the people of Brussels, the bar has a list of 90 fine beers—a perfect introduction to the world of Belgian beers.
5 Rue du Chêne, Brussels

TRAIL OR TOUR STATS
2 hours, plus drinking time
7 miles (10 km)

0   200 yards

0   200m

IN 'T SPINNEKOPKE
4 Away from Grand Place, but not too far, can be found In 't Spinnekopke. "The Little Spiders Head" is a small, intimate two-bar restaurant and café. It is as Bruxellois as you can get and has to be one of the best places in Brussels to eat and drink beer. Chef Jean Rodriguez prides himself on pairing food and beer superbly. *1 Place du Jardin aux Fleurs, Brussels*

DELIRIUM
5 Ilot Sacré is a clamor of medieval lanes and fish restaurants with outrageous menu boards, and energetic and sometimes insistent waiters trying to coerce people inside to dine. Down one such alley is Delirium. Don't wait at your table for service, go to the bar, which claims to stock more than 2,000 beers.
4a Impasse de la Fidélité, Brussels

MORTE SUBITE
6 Along the road is Galeries Royales St Hubert. Once the world's largest covered shopping mall, it leads the way to Morte Subite—a magnificent Art Nouveau bar, which is said to be the best surviving fin-de-siecle long bar in the world. Here is the place to try wildly fermented lambic or gueuze beers with a plate of *tête pressée* (brawn) or *kip kap* (pig cheeks). *7 Rue Montagne aux Herbes Potageres, Brussels*

BIER CIRCUS
7 Up the hill from Central Station is Bier Circus. This is the place to seek out beers from Belgium's growing band of artisanal brewers and experience the creative diversity of Belgian brewing. But take some friends with you—many of the beers are served only in 75cl bottles.
89 Rue de l'Enseignement, Brussels

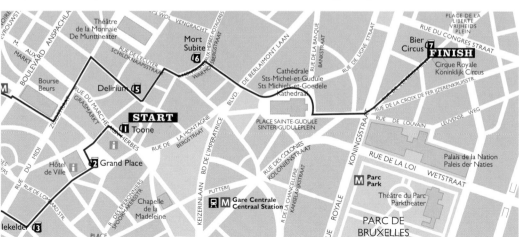

G R E A T

B E E R S

125

Duvel Moortgat

BELGIUM

Breendonkdorp 58-66,
B2870 Breendonk-Puurs,
www.duvel.be

Started as a small family brewery,
Moortgat continued producing
top-fermented ale at a time when
everywhere lager reigned. The
Moortgat ale evolved into the
iconoclastic Duvel, a beer that has
become so popular that the brewery
group renamed itself. Moortgat now
owns breweries in Belgium and abroad.

Duvel
BELGIAN STRONG ALE 8.5% ABV
Sometimes dubbed "red," to
distinguish it from the filtered
version, this ultra dry ale hides
its potency as no other.

Maredsous 8°
BROWN ABBEY ALE 8% ABV
Arguably the best from the
Maredsous Abbey range. Estery,
fruity notes, and tobacco leaf.

Eel River

USA

1777 Alamar Way
Fortuna, CA 95540,
www.eelriverbrewing.com

Eel River had been around less than five
years when, in 2000, it became the first
certified organic brewery in the US. The
brewpub added a production brewery in
nearby Scotia in 2007, moving into an
abandoned mill. The new brewery is 100
percent powered by biomass—that is,
mill waste such as wood chippings,
and spent grain from brewing.

Organic Porter
PORTER 6.3% ABV
Malty and creamy with chocolate
aromas and flavors, and lesser
notes of roast coffee beans. Robust.

Triple Exultation
OLD ALE 9.7% ABV
Not organic. A complex nose of
rich caramel-toffee and fruit,
then piney hops assert themselves.

127

Eggenberg

AUSTRIA

Eggenberg 1,
A-4655 Vorchdorf,
www.schloss-eggenberg.at

Schloss Eggenberg is a small castle in
Upper Austria that has been brewing
for more than 500 years. A broad
range of lagers (including a non-
alcoholic one) are produced for the
local market, and some fine bock beers
are brewed for export; these include
an urbock and even a blonde version of
the traditionally dark Samichlaus beer.

Samichlaus
DOPPELBOCK 14% ABV
Intense malt aroma, with noticeable
alcohol. Sweet and fruity (dried
cherries, figs, and plums); very
little hop character present.

Hopfenkönig
PILSNER 5.1% ABV
Very pale, with a firm head and
haylike spicy hop aromas. Light
body followed by some dry bitterness.

128

Eggenberg

CZECH REPUBLIC

Latrán 27, 38115, Český Krumlov,
www.eggenberg.cz

Nowhere but in Bohemia could two
towns merge over brewing disputes.
Years of arguing about wheat beer
privileges were resolved simply by
uniting neighbors Latrán and
Krumlov, and establishing a single
brewery. Over time, the brewery passed
from the Eggenberg family to the
Schwarzenbergs and down the
centuries to its present owners, Dionex.

Eggenberg Světlý Ležák
PREMIUM LAGER 5% ABV
Powerfully floral with sweet
butterscotch notes; zesty,
firm, and delightfully balanced
to a bitter finish.

Eggenberg Tmavý Ležák
DARK BEER 4.2% ABV
Deep and dark, with a hop
pungency, then a malty caramel
and toffee bittersweet palate.

129

Einbecker

GERMANY

Papenstr. 4, 37574 Einbeck,
www.einbecker.com

The story goes that, in 1521, Martin Luther said that Einbecker's beer was his favorite. In 1612, Bavarian dukes engaged a master brewer from Einbeck, whose beer eventually became known as bock, in a corruption of the name Einbeck.

Ur-Bock Hell
BOCK 6.5% ABV
The pale malt and fine hops give this classic bock a hearty taste.

Einbecker Spezial
EXPORT 5.2% ABV
Has the typical golden-yellow color of an export beer. Has a fine, slightly sweet flavor.

Emerson's Brewery

NEW ZEALAND

14 Wickliffe Street, Dunedin,
www.emersons.co.nz

New Zealand's most awarded micro offers an enviable portfolio of year-round beers, as well as seasonal specialties such as Taieri George, a spiced dark ale, and a US pale ale featuring American hops.

BREWING SECRET Emerson's delightful session beer called Bookbinder Bitter is available only on tap.

Emerson's Old 95
BARLEY WINE 7% ABV
Robust bottle conditioned ale, with rich, toffeelike malt and resiny hops. Will reward careful cellaring.

Emerson's Organic Pilsner
NEW WORLD PILSNER 4.9% ABV
Bursting with passion fruit and citrus. A showcase for New Zealand's Riwaka hop variety.

131

Erdinger

GERMANY

Lange Zeile 1+3,
85435 Erding,
www.erdinger.de

This is the biggest and most famous
specialist wheat beer brewery in the
world. The first mention of a brewery
at Erding was in 1886, but it was not
until 1949 that the name Erdinger
Weissbräu was used.

BREWING SECRET Fresh spring
water and hops from the Hallertau
region are used in brewing.

Erdinger Pikantus
DARK WEIZENBOCK 7.3% ABV
Normally a wheat bock is sweet,
but not so Erdinger's. Watch out
for the ABV on this one.

Erdinger Schneeweisse
WINTER BEER 5.6% ABV
Darker and heavier bodied than
the normal weizen. It is available
between October and February.

Everards

ENGLAND

Castle Acres, Narborough,
Leicestershire, LE19 1BY
www.everards.co.uk

After brewing his first pint in 1849,
William Everard stated his intention,
and one that the fifth-generation family
is proud to uphold: "No effort shall be
found wanting in the production and
supply of genuine ale of first-rate
quality." Integrity remains king today.

BREWING SECRET Fuggles and
Goldings are the key hops here.

Tiger
BITTER 4.2% ABV
Some spicy hop and caramel on
the nose. Classically bittersweet
palate, with a rounded toffeeness.

Original
STRONG BITTER 5.2% ABV
Copper-hued, full-bodied, and a
toasted caramel aroma beckoning
port wine and fruit flavors.

Exmoor

ENGLAND

Wiveliscombe,
Somerset, TA4 2NY
www.exmoorales.co.uk

Exmoor was among the first wave
of microbreweries in the early 1980s.
Its fundamentals have never altered
from a reliance on skills, investment
in innovation, and adherence to the
principles of small-batch brewing.
Being Somerset's largest brewery
positions it as a regional producer,
and the potential of its backbone brands
is still to be fully capitalized upon.

Exmoor Gold
BITTER 4.5% ABV
Powerful earthy hop, lemon,
and juicy malt aromas; fruity,
butterscotch sweetness, and
memorable finish.

Exmoor Ale
BITTER 3.8% ABV
Medium-bodied, with some malt
and hop in the aroma and bitter
hop aftertaste.

Fantôme

BELGIUM

8, Rue Préal,
B5454 Soy-Erezée,
www.fantome.be

Dany Prignon started this micro in
a shed in the Ardennes, and while
today he exports his beers to many
countries, the shed is still the brewery's
home—though it now contains far
more equipment.

BREWING SECRET More works
of art than products of brewing
science, many of the beers are
never brewed the same way twice.

Black Ghost
BELGIAN STRONG DARK ALE 8% ABV
One of the few regularly seen:
malty, with fruity depths, but
also flavors of cypress and pine.

Fantôme
SAISON 8% ABV
The brewery's staple blonde beer:
fruity, lactic, variable, and in the
style of a saison.

135

Fässla

GERMANY

Obere Königstr. 19-21,
6052 Bamberg,
www.faessla.de

In 1649, just a year after the end of
the Thirty Years' War, master brewer
Hans Lauer founded this brewery in
Bamberg. In modern times, 1986 was
a turning point, when the Kalb family
took over control. Fässla's specialty
beers are well known in the region.

BREWING SECRET Bambergator
is the strongest beer brewed in
Bamberg.

Lagerbier
LAGER 5.5% ABV
Strong yellow in color; fine,
compact foam; sparkling.
Full-bodied and slightly malty
with a light bitter taste.

Bambergator
DOPPELBOCK 8.5% ABV
A dark brown, full-bodied, and
very strong doppelbock, bursting
with harmonious hop bitters.

Faust

GERMANY

Hauptstr. 219,
63897 Miltenberg,
www.faust.de

A typical regional family-run company.
The brewery is about 350 years old and
changed hands many times in the first
200 years of its history. The Fausts
took over in 1895, and still own it
today. There are many different
styles of beer produced, some of
which have won prizes.

Schwarzviertler
DUNKEL 5.2% ABV
Dark, roasty, and slightly smoky.
There is also caramel and a little
bitter-chocolate on the tongue. It
is full-bodied and has a dry finish.

Faust Kräusen
KELLERBIER 5.5% ABV
A mild, full-bodied beer with a
light note of honey; it is very fresh.

137

Felinfoel

WALES

Llanelli, Carmarthenshire,
SA14 8LB
www.felinfoel-brewery.com

Sitting astride the Liedi River and
leaning heavily on the industrial
traditions of south Wales—and its
workers' thirsts—Felinfoel Brewery
has been in existence since 1878.
It is famed for producing Britain's
first canned beer in 1935. Extensive
modernization came in the 1970s,
but Felinfoel is still family-owned.

Double Dragon
BITTER **4.2% ABV**
Invitingly rich in color, malty and
subtly hopped, with an evenly
balanced, full-drinking nature.

Cambrian Bitter
BITTER **3.9% ABV**
Labeled "a good, honest Welsh
bitter," the bitter is full-flavored,
with balanced malt and hop aromas.

Fiege

GERMANY

Moritz Fiege, Scharnhorststr. 21-25,
44787 Bochum,
www.moritzfiege.de

"We are a classic regional brewery"
says Hugo Fiege, the boss of the
company. He sees his brewery as an
ambassador for the Ruhr region. It
is an institution offering typical local
beers—inhabitants of the Ruhr love
their beer. There is little chance of
a big global player acquiring Fiege.

Moritz Fiege Pils
PILSNER 4.9% ABV
A classic pilsner with bitter aromas
of good hops, a light malty taste,
and a fine dry structure.

Schwarzbier
SCHWARZBIER 4.9% ABV
Elegant and with a malty sweetness,
this coffee-colored beer has light
bitter aromas of fine hops.

Finlandia

FINLAND

Suokulmantie 237, Matku,
Forssa FI-31110,
www.finlandiasahti.fi

Finlandia is a specialist brewer of *sahti*,
a traditional Finnish home-brew made
with rye and other grains, flavored
with juniper twigs and berries. Beer
enthusiasts can sample Finlandia Sahti
in Helsinki at St. Urho's Pub and the
Restaurant Savotta. The best time to
do so is during Helsinki's Sahti Week,
which takes place in May each year.

Sahti Strong
SAHTI 10% ABV
Sweet and somewhat oily on
the palate; the juniper nose gives
way to a bubblegum aftertaste.

Tavallinen
SAHTI 8% ABV
A deep chestnut color, with
a heavy juniper nose and a
hint of blackcurrant.

Flensburger

GERMANY

Munketoft 12, 24937 Flensburg,
www.flensburger.de

Five citizens of Flensburg founded
this brewery in 1888. During the
1970s, the brewery's reputation
was enhanced when a comedian
kept referring to a "Flasch Flens"
in his act. The term came to be used
for a bottle of Flensburger, which at
the time was the only German beer
to use clip-top bottles.

Flensburger Pils
PILSNER 4.8% ABV
A typical golden pilsner—malty,
refreshing, and with slightly
bitter aromas of hops in the finish.

Kellerbier
KELLERBIER 4.8% ABV
Amber and cloudy, like all
kellerbiers, the Flensburger
version is full-bodied and tastes
naturally fresh, slightly sweet,
and has a dry finish.

141

Flossmoor Station

USA

1035 Sterling Avenue
Flossmoor, IL 60422,
www.flossmoorstation.com

Brewers Matt Van Wyk and Andrew
Mason have expanded on what barrel-
ageing pioneer Todd Ashman started
at Flossmoor Station Brewing. They
offer a wide range of award-winning
beers in a pub housed in a former
train station. The brewery recently
launched a small range of bottled beers.

Pullman Brown Ale
BROWN ALE 7% ABV
Brewed with hand-toasted malts
and molasses. A full-bodied blend
of chocolate, toffee, and dark fruit.

De Wilde Zuidentrein
SOUR ALE 7% ABV
A Flanders brown ale, aged
in an oak wine barrel on fresh
raspberries for a year, dosed
with wild yeasts.

142

Flying Dog

USA

2401 Blake Street
Denver, CO 80205,
www.flyingdogales.com

With labels by British illustrator Ralph
Steadman, and the "gonzo" spirit of the
late Hunter S. Thompson (both friends
of founder George Stranahan), Flying
Dog is not your average brewery.
The original brewpub was founded
in Aspen but is now headquartered
in Denver, while the company moved
brewing operations to Frederick in
Maryland in 2008.

Gonzo Imperial Porter
PORTER 9% ABV
Rummy, chocolatey, and almost
sweet before dry cocoa flavors
and solid hop bitterness kick in.

Doggie Style Pale Ale
PALE ALE 5.3% ABV
A fragrant mixture of fresh fruits
to start. Citrus accentuates fruit
in the middle, well balanced by
biscuity malt. Clean, dry finish.

Flying Fish

USA

1940 Olney Avenue
Cherry Hill, NJ 08003,
www.flyingfish.com

Flying Fish Brewing began worldwide and then went local. It started out as a "virtual brewery" on the Internet before establishing itself as a distinctly regional brewery in 1996, now serving a 100-mile (160-km) radius around its South Jersey home. The brewery recently increased capacity, with plans to widen the range of beers on offer.

Belgian Style Dubbel
DOUBLE 7% ABV
Chocolate mingled with dark fruit, and a pleasant whiff of alcohol. Finishes on the sweet side of dry.

ESB Ale
EXTRA SPECIAL BITTER 5.5% ABV
Malt-accented, rich with caramel and fruit character, and with an underlying nuttiness. Hops are American, but restrained.

Forstner

AUSTRIA

Dorfstrasse 52,
A-8401 Kalsdorf bei Graz,
www.hofbraeu.at

One of the more adventurous new
brewers, Gerhard Forstner has recently
made inroads into brewing Belgian and
American-style ales. His brewery is in
an old farmhouse building that has also
served as a school. Some of his beers are
endorsed by the Slow Food movement
and are sold at Slow Food festivals.

Styrian Ale
BITTER ALE 5.6% ABV
Very dark burgundy; roasty and
fruity (grapefruit?) aromas;
slightly tart and very refreshing,
with a medium bitterness.

Triple 22
BELGIAN STYLE TRIPLE 9.5% ABV
Copper, with firm head and aroma
of pawpaw and mango. Sweet and
full-bodied; spicy and bitter finish.

145

Freeminer

ENGLAND

Cinderford, Gloucestershire,
GL14 3JA
www.freeminer.com

Anyone born in the Forest of Dean who
has worked in a coal mine for a year
and a day may open his own mine.
Few such mines remain, but Freeminer
celebrates this heritage with its ales.

BREWING SECRET Freeminer
ales are made from traditional
malt varieties and whole
Worcestershire hops in
open-topped fermenters.

Speculation
STRONG BITTER 4.8% ABV
An initial chocolate sweetness
is replaced by a hoppy rush
and rich malt flavor layer.

Freeminer Bitter
STRONG BITTER 4.8% ABV
Distinctly bitter and abundantly
hoppy, balanced by a malt
character that denotes
"no-nonsense" beer.

Freiberger

GERMANY

Am Fürstenwald, 09599 Freiberg,
www.freiberger-bier.de

This brewery was the first in Sachsen
to produce a pilsner. Other exclusive
beers followed: Freiberger Silberquell
(1903) and a wheat beer (1909). The
Eichbaum brewery in Mannheim has
acquired Freiberger and is focusing
on making it one of the most modern
beer producers in Germany.

Jubiläums-Festbier
MÄRZEN 5.8% ABV
With aromas of malt and a very
fine taste of hops, this amber-
colored beer is pleasant and
full-bodied.

Schwarzes Bergbier
SCHWARZBIER 4.7% ABV
Deep black, with fresh, malty
aromas. Full-bodied and precisely
balanced between malts and hops.

Friedenfels

GERMANY

Schlossbrauerei Friedenfels,
Gemmingenstr. 33, 95688 Friedenfels,
www.schlossbrauerei-friedenfels.de

The brewery is situated in the southern
part of the largest forest in Europe,
between Oberpfälzer Wald and
Fichtelgebirge. Friedenfels is the
leading brewery of the region.

BREWING SECRET The pure
springs of the national park
have helped Friedenfels to
produce excellent beers for
more than 100 years.

Friedenfelser Pils Leicht
LIGHT BEER 2.8% ABV
This reduced-alcohol beer is golden
and on the dry side, with aromas
of fine hops in the finish.

Friedenfelser Weizen Leicht
LIGHT WHEAT BEER 2.7% ABV
This light beer is fermented in the
bottle. Its taste is a mixture of bitter
hops and sweet barley and wheat—
typical of the style.

Freistädter

AUSTRIA

Promenade 7, A-4240 Freistadt,
www.freistaedter-bier.at

The town of Freistadt lies close to
Austria's border with the Czech
Republic, and its brewery is owned
by the townspeople. Since 1777 every
owner of a building inside the old city
walls automatically owns a certain
number of shares of the brewery;
those shares can be sold only along
with the building itself.

Rauchbier
SMOKED LAGER 5.3% ABV
Pale amber, with a smoky nose;
dry and aromatic, with a nice
balance of smoked malt and hops.

Ratsherrn Trunk
EXPORT 5.1% ABV
A firm head and a full body.
Low hop bitterness, with a
hint of grass in the aftertaste.

Füchschen

GERMANY

Ratinger Str. 28, 40213 Düsseldorf,
www.fuechschen.de

Altbier has been a favored brew at
Füchschen since 1848. The fourth
generation of the family is in charge.
There have been some changes since
1995, including the installation of
new brewing equipment.

BREWING SECRET The Düsseldorf
carnival in February is a good
opportunity to sample the altbier.

Füchschen Alt
ALTBIER 4.5% ABV
Dark mahogany in color, this typical
Düsseldorfer is malty with a very
intense aroma of hops. Slightly
carbonated, and fresh.

Silberfüchsen
WHEAT BEER 5.4% ABV
A northern-style wheat beer, less
sweet than its Bavarian counterpart.
Smooth, fruity, and sparkling.

Fuller's

ENGLAND

Chiswick Lane South, London,
W4 2QB
www.fullers.co.uk

London's last remaining traditional
family brewer, Fuller's has been based
at the historic Griffin Brewery near the
Thames River in Chiswick since 1845.
Brewing on the site, however, goes
back 350 years. Despite its global
prominence, Fuller's retains a small
company spirit and formidably
energetic outlook. Its beers have
received countless awards, notably the
Campaign For Real Ale Champion Beer
of Britain, which it has won five times.

London Pride
BITTER 4.1% ABV
A fruity sweet malt nose and
a floral spiced hop presence
with marmalade undercurrents.

ESB
EXTRA SPECIAL BITTER 5.5% ABV
Complex aromas, with the house-
style orange fruit complementing
tangy hops and roasted malt.

151

Full Sail

USA

506 Columbia Street
Hood River, OR 97031,
www.fullsailbrewing.com

Full Sail represents much that is
new in American brewing. Founded
in 1987, it became employee-owned
in 1999, and its beers reflect an
independent nature. The core brands
(Amber, IPA, and Pale Ale) reach a
wide audience in 15 western states.

BREWING SECRET The brewery
also offers seasonals that bear the
LTD (Living the Dream) label and
a bolder series of Brewmaster's
Reserve beers throughout the year.

Amber
AMBER ALE 5.5% ABV
Citrus and spice, quickly balanced
by underlying sweetness. Seamless
through to a clean finish.

Session Lager
US LAGER 5.1% ABV
Designed as a throwback to beer
produced before Prohibition, with
appropriately retro packaging.
Clean and malt-accented.

Fürstenberg

GERMANY

Postplatz 1-4, 78166
Donaueschingen,
www.fuerstenberg.de

Count Heinrich I von Fürstenberg was
granted the right to brew beer in 1283,
but it was not until 300 years later
that a proper brewery was built.
Fürstenberg was a major brewery
by the beginning of the 20th century.

BREWING SECRET The beers
are made with water from the
Black Forest and yeast from
Donaueschingen.

Fürstenberg Gold
LAGER 4.9% ABV
Smooth, with few aromas of hops.
This clear golden beer is a bit
sweeter than the usual lager.

Fürstenberg Hefe Dunkel
DUNKEL 5.4% ABV
Chestnut in color, and sparkling;
harmonious with a malty aroma
and light caramel sweetness, yet
strong in the mouth.

153

Fürstlichen Ellingen

GERMANY

Schloss-Strasse 19, 91792 Ellingen,
www.fuerst-carl.de

Owner Carl Friedrich Fürst von Wrede
is a direct descendant of Napoleon's field
marshal Carl Philipp, Prince of Wrede.
The brewery opposite his castle in
Ellingen was founded in 1690, but the
brewing history of Ellingen is certainly
older. The beer has been called Fürst
Carl for about 200 years.

Fürst Carl Josefi Bock
BOCK 7% ABV
A creamy, malty, and full-bodied
beer, with a velvet and silky texture.

Fürst Carl Urhell
LAGER 4.6% ABV
The clear yellow color is typical for a
lager; the taste is pleasant and not
too dry, with very little sweetness.

Galbraith's

NEW ZEALAND

2 Mt. Eden Road, Mt. Eden,
Auckland,
www.alehouse.co.nz

Located in a former library, New
Zealand's first real ale brewpub is
best known for its home-brewed
English style ales—all served by
hand pump. Visitors can also enjoy
an excellent Abbey-style ale and a
couple of flavorsome lagers, as well
as a fine range of imports and craft
beers from other New Zealand brewers.

Bellringers Bitter
ENGLISH BEST BITTER 4.5% ABV
Copper colored ale with a biscuity,
toffeelike palate, plenty of earthy
hops, and an appetizingly dry finish.

Bob Hudson's Bitter
ENGLISH BITTER 4% ABV
A full-flavored session bitter very
much in the vein of the English
pale ale Timothy Taylor's Landlord.

Gayant

FRANCE

63 Faubourg de Paris,
59500 Douai,
www.brasseurs-gayant.com

Established in 1919, this independent,
family-owned brewery has always
embraced and pioneered new styles
of brewing, from ales made using
the top-fermentation technique, to
Celta, the first non-alcoholic beer.

BREWING SECRET Brasseurs
de Gayant brews the strongest
beer in France, called Bière du
Démon (12% ABV).

La Goudale
ALE 7.2% ABV
Golden, dense, and full of malty
aromas, with a slight bitterness
imbued by the Flemish hops.

Amadeus
WHEAT BEER 4.5% ABV
Cloudy and pale yellow, this
is a light and refreshing beer,
with aromas of citrus fruit
and coriander.

Gilde

GERMANY

Hildesheimer Str. 132,
Hanover,
www.gildebrau.de

It was about 500 years ago that Cord
Broyhan presented his beer to the
people of Hanover. *Broyhan*—a pale
style of wheat beer—was popular for
centuries in the city. Gilde, Hanover's
longest-surviving brewery, now owned
by InBev, was founded in 1870.

BREWING SECRET A modern
version of broyhan is exported
to the US.

Ratskeller Premium Pils
PILSNER 4.9% ABV
A dry, golden-yellow pilsner;
full-bodied, typical bitterness
of hops, and a nice finish.

Lindener Special
EXPORT 5.1% ABV
The most successful export beer of
Niedersachsen has a golden color
and tastes pleasant with smooth
yeast-flower flavors in the mouth.

Girardin

BELGIUM

Lindeberg 10-12,
1700 Sint-Ulriks-Kapelle,
www.brouwerijgirardin.com

As rural as you can get, Girardin is
still very much a farm and brewery,
and this authentic lambic brewer and
gueuze blender has no time for curious
visitors. If, however, you come simply
to stock up on lambic—as the locals
and other blenders do—the brewers
will gladly help you to their citrussy,
spontaneously fermented brews.

Faro Girardin
BLENDED LAMBIC 5% ABV
Caramel, meaty, and woody
aromas; slight sour edge around
the caramel. Filtered, as the
yeast would wreak havoc
with sugars from the syrup.

Girardin Fond Gueuze
GUEUZE 5% ABV
This delectable unfiltered gueuze
has a marked grapefruit flavor.

Glaab

GERMANY

Frankfurter Str. 9,
63500 Seligenstadt,
www.glaabsbraeu.de

For more than 250 years this brewery
has been owned by the Glaab family.
It was founded in 1744 and became
known for its wide variety of beers
and for Vitamalz, the biggest German
brand of pure malt drinks. The
company is the only private brewery
in the Offenbach region, to the south
of Frankfurt.

1744
KELLERBIER 5.3% ABV
This cloudy, amber-colored beer
is Glaab's youngest product.
The taste of fine malt is typical.

Dunkles
DUNKEL 5.3% ABV
Clear amber-colored beer in which
the light bitterness of hops is
prominent. A great dunkel
with a nice malty finish.

Goose Island

USA

1800 West Fulton Street
Chicago, IL 60612,
www.gooseisland.com

This brewery's extensive range reflects
the MBA (Master of Beer Appreciation)
Program that it established shortly after
opening as a brewpub in 1988. When Goose
Island built its production brewery in 1995,
brewmaster Greg Hall would launch dozens
of styles during the course of a year. Goose
Island still operates the original pub on
Clybourn as well as another near Wrigley
Field, and both still offer an "MBA"
(actually a kind of loyalty card!).

India Pale Ale
INDIA PALE ALE 5.9% ABV
Pineapple and grapefruit, full of
hop flavor, with a fruit and malt
back-bone balancing the bitterness.

312 Urban Wheat
US WHEAT BEER 4.2% ABV
Typically unfiltered and hazy,
with a citrussy, almost sweet,
hop nose that announces it is
American. Tart, fruity, with
underlying creaminess.

Gourmet-bryggeriet

DENMARK

ytoften 10-12,
DK-4000 Roskilde,
www.gourmetbryggeriet.dk

One of the largest microbreweries
in Denmark, "The Gourmet Brewery"
creates specialty beers that are designed
to be paired with food. The brewery's
partner is a trained chef who works
together with a local restaurant to create
recipes that are attached to 66cl bottles
for sharing. The company recently
acquired the Ølfabrikken Brewery.

Ølfabrikken Porter
PORTER 7.5% ABV
Black as the night, with a thick
head of foam. Intense body with
coffee, chocolate, and liquorice
notes.

Gourmetbryggeriet Bock
DOPPELBOCK 7.2% ABV
Deep reddish in color, with a
heavy aroma of malt and caramel
backing up the strong body.

Great Divide

USA

2201 Arapahoe Street
Denver, CO 80205,
www.greatdivide.com

Opened in 1994, Great Divide Brewing
quickly earned a reputation for
carefully balanced beers. Its ales have
grown bigger (in strength and hop
character), and the brewery's reputation
has grown, but its beers still retain that
delicate equilibrium. The brewery is
a short walk from Coors Field, home
of the Rockies baseball team.

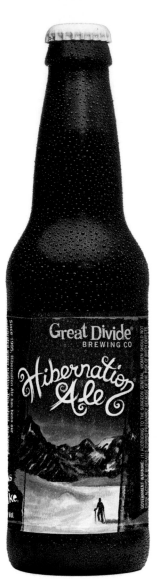

Hibernation Ale
OLD ALE 8.1% ABV
A complex, earthy nose packed with
chocolate, roasted nuts, and freshly
baked molasses cookies—flavors
just keep emerging.

Titan IPA
INDIA PALE ALE 6.8% ABV
Balanced, in a big way, with plenty
of caramel-sweet body to match the
piney, grapefruity hops throughout.

Great Lakes

USA

2516 Market Avenue
Cleveland, OH 44113,
www.greatlakesbrewing.com

Selling its beer across a growing region, this brewery has been an industry leader in tracking the quality of its beer on retailers' shelves. Its brewing complex always merits a visit. The original 1988 brewpub sits across from the production brewery, which came online in 1998. Visitors are directed to the taproom's striking Tiger Mahogany bar and shown bullet holes reputedly made by Eliot Ness, the "untouchable" Prohibition agent who brought down gangster Al Capone.

Edmund Fitzgerald Porter
PORTER 5.8% ABV
Perfectly balanced, chocolate-mocha throughout, delightful fresh quality, and a dry coffee finish.

Eliot Ness
VIENNA LAGER 6.2% ABV
Bold and hoppy in the Vienna style, with creamy, nutty maltiness and brisk hoppiness nicely balanced.

G

Green Flash

USA

1430 Vantage Court
Vista, CA 92081,
www.greenflashbrew.com

Green Flash refers to a rare light
phenomenon that lasts only seconds
at sunrise or sunset over water. Green
seems appropriate for a brewery gaining
a national reputation for its hop-accented
beers, although brewer Chuck Silva has
proved adept at a wide range of styles.

West Coast IPA
INDIA PALE ALE 7% ABV
Northwest hops balanced on a
solid malt base. Earthy, floral,
citrussy, piney, grapefruity,
and bitter.

Nut Brown Ale
BROWN ALE 5.5% ABV
Deep brown, with nuts and
cocoa from the outset, and more
chocolate and caramel on the
palate. Subdued, earthy hops.

Greene King

ENGLAND

Bury St. Edmunds,
Suffolk, IP33 1QT
www.greeneking.co.uk

After more than 200 years, Greene King has developed into a formidable and dynamic force in the British brewing industry. Benjamin Greene opened his brewery in 1799 and it merged with the rival King Brewery in 1887. The company has in recent years acquired several of its competitors—namely, Morland, Ruddles, Ridley's, and Hardy & Hanson—and closed them amid some controversy. Belhaven of Dunbar was another recent acquisition, it being bought up in 2005.

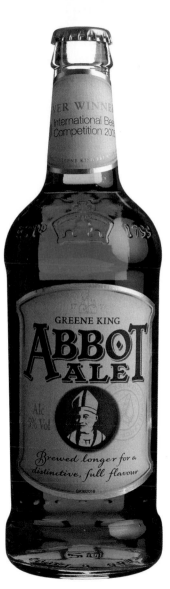

Abbot Ale
STRONG BITTER 5% ABV
A biscuit malt and spicy hop aroma, with a tangy and bittersweet fruit and malt palate.

IPA
INDIA PALE ALE 3.6% ABV
Distinctly copper-colored, with a clean, fresh hop savoriness and subtle, sweetish malty nose.

Grünbach

GERMANY

Kellerberg 2, 85461 Bockhorn,
www.schlossbrauerei-gruenbach.de

Grünbach has had a host of owners,
including the famous Paulaner and
Erdinger breweries. Alexander Noll
is currently at the helm.

BREWING SECRET Grünbach's
Benno Scharl wheat beer carries
the name of an 18th-century
Bavarian master brewer who
wrote an influential textbook
on brewing techniques.

Altweizen Gold
WHEAT BEER 5.3% ABV
Clear golden and finely balanced
between yeast and carbonic
acid, with a lightly sparkling,
dry freshness.

Benno Scharl
WHEAT BEER 5.3% ABV
Yellow, and clouded with yeast,
Benno Scharl tastes mild and
sweet, pleasant and well balanced.

Guinness

IRELAND

St. James's Gate, Dublin 8,
www.guinness.com

When you can make a virtue out of
the time it takes to pour a pint—119.5
seconds to be precise—you know you
have no ordinary beer in your hands.
Guinness defines stout, Ireland, and
Irishness, but it is also inextricably
linked with innovation in physics,
chemistry, packaging, and
advertising. 250 years after
young Arthur Guinness's first
mash, it is brewed in 50 countries
worldwide and enjoyed in 150.

Guinness Original
STOUT 4.2% ABV
The packaged version's coffee
and cream aroma highlights
fruit, chocolate, and some
late hoppiness.

Foreign Extra Stout
SPECIAL STOUT 7.5% ABV
Leafy hop aroma, with burnt
toast, rich malt, bitter coffee,
and liquorice flavors ripening
effortlessly.

Haake-Beck

GERMANY

Am Deich 18/19,
28365 Bremen,
www.haake-beck.de

Founded in 1826, the Haake-Beck
brewery is one of the most famous
in northern Germany. Milestones in
the company's history include the
creation of Haake-Beck Kräusen
Pils and the first Maibock in 1950.
It is part of the InBev stable today.

BREWING SECRET Haake-Beck's
sister is the famous Beck's label,
which is exported by InBev around
the world.

Haake-Beck 12
EXPORT 5% ABV
This is a new Haake-Beck.
A harmonious, golden beer,
with a level of sweetness that is
often liked by women drinkers.

Edel Hell
LAGER 4.7% ABV
A mild alternative to the pilsner:
not so dry, a little bit sweet, and
golden like a typical lager.

Haandbryggeriet

NORWAY

Thornegaten 39,
N-3015 Drammen,
www.haandbryggeriet.net

This small brewery is known for its hand-made brews and for keeping Norwegian brewing traditions alive. Housed in a 200-year-old wooden building, it is run by volunteers, and experimentation is encouraged.

BREWING SECRET As well as using old oak wine barrels, they are now ageing beer in former Akevitt spirit casks.

Dark Force
WHEAT STOUT 9% ABV
Uses wheat and dark roasted malts and house wheat yeast. High hop aroma and ample bitterness.

Norwegian Wood
TRADITIONAL ALE 6.5% ABV
Made from naturally smoked Munich, Crystal, and chocolate malts; spiced with locally gathered juniper twigs and berries.

169

Hacker-Pschorr

GERMANY

Hochstr. 75, 81541 München,
www.hacker-pschorr.de

Hacker-Pschorr is one of the most
traditional breweries in Munich, and
its restaurant is a tourist attraction,
especially during Oktoberfest. Beer
production was mentioned for the
first time here in 1417.

BREWING SECRET The Purity
Law and principles of long
lagering are followed; there
are no preservatives or additives.

1417
KELLERBIER 5.5% ABV
Naturally cloudy, unfiltered, with
a dull golden color. Low carbonic
acid makes it very smooth.

Superior
MÜNCHNER SPECIAL 6% ABV
The clear, amber-colored Superior
is based on an old recipe and has a
malty, aromatic taste, without too
many hops. Highly drinkable.

Hair of the Dog

USA

4509 Southeast 23rd Avenue
Portland, OR 97202,
www.hairofthedog.com

Chef-turned-brewer Alan Sprints
founded this tiny cult brewery in
1994. His first ale, Adam, was brewed
in the Adambier style of Dortmund
in Germany, and based on the research
of beer writer Fred Eckhardt.

BREWING SECRET Every bottle
carries a batch number. Check the
website to match it to brewing and
bottling dates.

Adam
STRONG ALE 10% ABV
Rich and complex, with dark
fruits, bread, chocolate, smoked
peat, and more, all cleverly unified.

Fred
STRONG ALE 10% ABV
Named after Eckhardt, this beer
defies categorization. Dark fruits
and juicy ones, spices and hops—
impossible to summarize.

Hakusekikan

JAPAN

5251-1 Hirukawa Tahara,
Nagatsugawa, Gifu 509-8301,
www.hakusekikan-beer.jp

One of Japan's most distinctive
breweries, Hakusekikan pushes the
envelope of possible beer styles. Head
brewer Satoshi Niwa is brilliant and
imaginative, experimenting with wild
beers using airborne yeast, while also
making use of long fermentation times,
barrel ageing, and other methods to
produce truly distinctive beers.

Super Vintage
STRONG ALE 14.3% ABV
Astonishingly fruity and complex
beer, yet boasts a surprisingly dry
finish. Permanently on tap at Beer
Club Popeye in Tokyo.

Smoked Pale Ale
PALE ALE 5% ABV
A session pale ale given just a hint
of smoked malt, with the smoky
flavor appearing only in the finish.

Hambleton

ENGLAND

Holme-on-Swale,
North Yorkshire, YO7 4JE
www.hambletonales.co.uk

A million-pound investment has resulted in a completely new brewery for Hambleton, with state-of-the-art bottling facilities. Innovation has been at the heart of the operation since 1991, as evident in the label designs and bespoke brewing equipment. Several awards, including one for a gluten-free range, have been well deserved.

Stallion
BITTER 4.2% ABV
For some, a true Yorkshire bitter, with its malty character, nuttiness, and enhanced hopping rate.

Nightmare
PORTER 5% ABV
An extra-stout porter that uses a combination of four malts for a massively complex flavor.

Harpoon

USA

306 Northern Avenue
Boston, MA 02210,
www.harpoonbrewery.com

This brewery, with major facilities in
Boston and Vermont, has tapped into
specialty-beer-drinkers' affection for
hops, with its flagship IPA accounting
for 60 percent of sales. However, its
wheat-based UFO has recently been
the fastest-growing brand, and its 100
Barrel Series of one-offs guarantees
there's always something new.

IPA
INDIA PALE ALE 5.9% ABV
Floral at the outset; zestful citrus
aromas. More hops in the flavor,
biscuitlike palate, subdued
bitterness at the end.

Munich Dark
DUNKEL 5.5% ABV
Rich, almost sweet, with hints of
toast, then chocolate. Restrained
hops and a long, smooth finish.

Harvey's

ENGLAND

Lewes, East Sussex,
BN7 2AH
www.harveys.org.uk

The seventh generation of John
Harvey's descendants are still involved
in this prime example of Victorian
Gothic-style brewery grandeur. The
tower and brewhouse dominate the
skyline, and the fermenting rooms
and cellars remain structurally
unaltered, although they now house
a modern plant with equipment that
has increased production enormously.

Blue Label
PALE ALE 3.6% ABV
Deliciously full-bodied though
fairly low in alcohol, with a
whiff of leafy hop and sweet
malt counterbalance.

Armada Ale
BEST BITTER 4.5% ABV
Amber colored, with a well-
balanced combination of fruit
and hops on the palate.

Harviestoun

SCOTLAND

Alva, Clackmannanshire,
FK12 5DQ
www.harviestoun-brewery.co.uk

The brewers of Harviestoun say they
can't pretend it's a job—it's their work,
but also their play and their passion.
Curiosity toward flavors and aromas
wrung from natural ingredients was
the brewery's mission in 1985, when
the business was originally set up,
and a move to a purpose-built plant
with fresh investment has resulted
in national accolades.

Bitter & Twisted
BITTER 4.2% ABV
Ripe grapefruit and lemon-
influenced hop aromas are
anchored by a distinct maltiness.

Schiehallion
PREMIUM LAGER 4.8% ABV
Cask lager, brewed with Bavarian
hops for a delightful nose. A rigid
maltiness prevails throughout.

Hawkshead

ENGLAND

Staveley, Cumbria,
LA8 9LR
www.hawksheadbrewery.co.uk

The focus at Hawkshead is on
traditional beer styles that have been
given a modern twist. A new 20-barrel
(3,200-liter) brewhouse was fitted out
in 2006—an integral feature is a farm
gate for leaning on contemplatively.
The brewery's public beer hall, where
award-winning ales are served, is a
magnificent showcase for the beers
and their provenance.

Hawkshead Red
RED ALE 4.2% ABV
A bittersweet red ale, malty
and spicy on the palate,
with juicy, woody aromas.

Hawkshead Gold
BEST BITTER 4.4% ABV
Hoppy and uncompromisingly
bitter, with complex fruit flavors
from its English and American
hop blend.

177

Herold

CZECH REPUBLIC
262 72 Březnice,
www.heroldbeer.com

The town's Baroque castle is fully restored, and its attached brewery continues to produce pilsner-style beers in a traditional, hand-crafted manner to a "small is beautiful" philosophy. The range includes wheat beers and Bohemian Black Lager.

BREWING SECRET Open fermenters, home-drawn water, and resident maltings accentuate its heritage.

Bohemian Black Lager
DARK LAGER 4.1% ABV
A schwarzbier-type lager; bitter chocolate flavors, plus a little malty sweetness, and a long, dry, slightly smoky finish.

Premium Bohemian Lager
PREMIUM LAGER 5.1% ABV
Full-bodied, yet softly textured, with a classic creamy malt veil and late hop dryness.

Herrngiersdorf

GERMANY

Schlossallee 5,
84097 Herrngiersdorf,
www.schlossbrauerei-
herrngiersdorf.de

Herrngiersdorf is situated between
Regensburg and Landhut, in the
middle of Niederbayern. With more
than 875 years of history behind it,
this is the oldest private brewery in
the world. It has been owned by the
Pausinger family since 1899. Since
1995 the sixth generation of the
family has been managing it.

Sündenbock
BOCK 7.3% ABV
A typical dark doppelbock with
a light taste of caramel; very
full-bodied and sweet in the finish.

Publiner
DUNKEL 4.9% ABV
This beer is very dark and has a
strong taste, with very roasty malt
aromas and light bitters of hops.
(The Irish would love it...)

High Falls

USA

445 St. Paul Street
Rochester, NY 14605,
www.highfalls.com

High Falls is still brewing old-style
Genesee beers on the site where they
have been made since 1878. It also
makes the J.W. Dundee family of
beers for the traditional ale market.

BREWING SECRET High Falls
is one of the largest and oldest
continuously operating breweries
in the US.

Genesee Cream Ale
CREAM ALE **4.9%** ABV
Pale, faintly sweet, with roast corn
flavors; smooth and easy to drink.

JW Dundee's IPA
INDIA PALE ALE **6.3%** ABV
A seasonal summer beer. Relatively
sweet caramel character, with
more bitterness than flavor
from its hops. Crisp finish.

Hoegaarden

BELGIUM

Stoopkensstraat 46,
B3320 Hoegaarden,
www.inbev.com

Although this is now a brand in the
portfolio of brewing giant InBev, it
is the lifeblood and spirit of Pierre
Celis, Belgium's preeminent brewing
revolutionary, that still haunts this
brewery. Proof of this came in 2007,
when InBev's moguls wanted to close
the plant: fate, however, obliged them
to reverse their decision.

Hoegaarden Wit
WITBIER 4.9% ABV
From as early as the 18th
century, the town of Hoegaarden
was importing blue Curaçao
oranges. The peel was mixed
with coriander seeds, and, as the
rich soil of the area yielded lots
of wheat, a very distinct, fruity,
and spicy style of beer evolved.

Hofbräu München

GERMANY

Hofbräuallee 1,
81829 München,
www.hofbraeuhaus.com

The Hofbräuhaus in Munich is
a very famous restaurant, frequented
by visitors from around the world. It
was founded in 1607 by Maximilian I,
Duke of Bavaria. The linked brewery
is situated in Riem, outside of the city.

BREWING SECRET The water
used to brew Hofbräu is drawn
from a depth of 490 ft (150 m).

Hofbräu Original
MÜNCHNER HELLES 5.1% ABV
This clear golden beer is
refreshing and dry, with
a harmonious balance of
malt and hops.

Hofbräu Dunkel
DUNKEL 5.5% ABV
This is the oldest type of
Bavarian beer, dark amber in
color, and full of fine flavor
and enticing malt aromas.

Hog's Back

ENGLAND

Tongham, Surrey,
GU10 1DE
www.hogsback.co.uk

Established in 1992, the Hog's Back brewhouse takes up part of an 18th-century farm. Steady expansion, extensions to storage facilities, and re-equipping the fermenting room have continued since, and many awards have been gathered along the way.

BREWERY SECRETS "Late hops" are added at the end of the boil, contributing additional fragrance to the beer.

Traditional English Ale / TEA
BEST BITTER **4.2% ABV**
Well-crafted, with delicate, fruity aromas, some bittersweet malt flavoring, and a long, dry finish.

Hog's Back Bitter
BITTER **3.7% ABV**
A biscuit-influenced session bitter, with a fragrantly aromatic citrus fruit and light malt afterglow.

183

Holden's

ENGLAND

Woodsetton, Dudley,
West Midlands, DY1 4LW
www.holdensbrewery.co.uk

Third and fourth-generation family
members are very much involved
in the Holden's business, which
started life in the 1920s with a
brewpub, before expanding next door
into a neatly tiled brewery on two floors.

BREWING SECRET The mild
uses a mix of amber malt,
caramalt, and black malt,
along with Fuggles hops.

Holden's Golden
BITTER 3.9% ABV
Fuggles hops and Maris Otter
malt combine in this medium-
bodied, straw-hued pale ale.

Black Country Mild
MILD 3.7% ABV
Bold chestnut red, with nutty
biscuit notes and wrappings
of chocolate, caramel, and
earthy hops.

Holt

ENGLAND

Cheetham,
Manchester, M3 1JD
www.joseph-holt.com

A family business survivor in an
increasingly corporate sector, Holt's
admits—with some pride—to being
unashamedly old-fashioned. That does
not mean backward-looking, however,
and its well-structured projects and
clear vision have brought steady
expansion to the brewery and to
its portfolio of 127 pubs.

Holt 1849
BEST BITTER 4.5% ABV
A 150-year anniversary ale,
with a vibrant and generous
celebratory hop flavor to match.

Holt Bitter
BITTER 4% ABV
Spicy hops dominate the aroma
with tart fruitiness tempered by
biscuit malt and bittersweet fruit.

Hook Norton

ENGLAND

Banbury, Oxfordshire,
OX15 5NY
www.hooky.co.uk

A particularly striking example of a
Victorian tower brewery, Hook Norton
is partly powered by steam, via a series
of belts, cogs, and shafts. Drays pulled
by shire horses deliver to local pubs,
further demonstrating how the
brewery likes to preserve traditional
practices. While doing this, Hook
Norton also produces some of the
country's most outstanding ales.

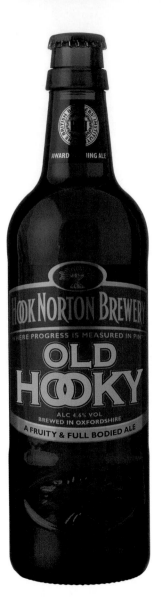

Old Hooky
STRONG BITTER 4.6% ABV
Beautifully poised, with a piquant,
fruity nature and malt character
rounding off a bitter finish.

Hooky Bitter
BITTER 3.6% ABV
Subtly hoppy on the nose,
then malt and fruit appear,
before a returning hop finish.

Hop Back

ENGLAND

Downton, Salisbury,
Wiltshire, SP5 3HU
www.hopback.co.uk

Having soon outgrown its humble
1980s pub-cellar beginnings at the
Wyndham Arms in Salisbury, Hop
Back developed and expanded through
a series of premises for brewing and
drinking its beers, picking up
significant awards along the way.
At the core of the range is the multi-
award-winning Summer Lightning.

Summer Lightning
STRONG BITTER 5% ABV
Intensely bitter, with a grassy,
fresh, hoppy aroma and some
malt lingering on the palate.

Crop Circle
BITTER 4.2% ABV
Cleverly blended aroma and
bittering hops combine with
corn nuances for a delicate
fruity crispness.

187

COTSWOLDS, ENGLAND

The village of Hook Norton in north Oxfordshire is the perfect base for any visitor exploring the Cotswolds or the city of Oxford. For the traveler, three of the village's pubs—the Sun, the Pear Tree, and the Gate Hangs High—all offer accommodation.

1 DAY 1: HOOK NORTON BREWERY
This is a near-perfect example of a Victorian tower brewery. It is still powered by a steam engine, and the making of Hook Norton's beers is a tactile, aural, and visual experience. Only the finest malted barley is used in the mash tun, and this needs to be manually removed when the wort is drained off the grist. The seemingly magical transformation of turning sweet wort into alcohol takes place in the brewery's hard-working open fermenters. A horse-drawn dray still delivers beer to local pubs. The Visitor Center is open from Monday to Saturday, though tours of the brewery must be booked beforehand via the website. The tour is followed by some sampling of Hook Norton beer.
Brewery Lane, Hook Norton (www.hooky.co.uk)

2 DAY 2: WYCHWOOD BREWERY
The drive from Hook Norton to Witney takes in some glorious countryside, and at the end of the trip is the Wychwood Brewery. Tours of the brewery can be booked online. They last for two hours and go through the brewing process for Wychwood and Brakspear beers, from raw ingredients to the finished product. The tour takes in Brakspear's famous "Double Drop system" fermenting vessels.
Eagle Maltings, The Crofts, Witney (www.wychwood.co.uk)

3 THE KING'S HEAD INN
Before returning to Hook Norton, pass by Cotswold Brewing (www.cotswoldbrewing company.com) at Foscot. Unusually for a British micro, brewer Richard Keene makes continental-style lagers. With a meandering stream at its side, the King's Head Inn, at nearby Bledington, is the perfect place to drink a glass of Cotswold Brewing's beer. *The King's Head Inn, The Green, Bledington (www.thekingsheadinn.net)*

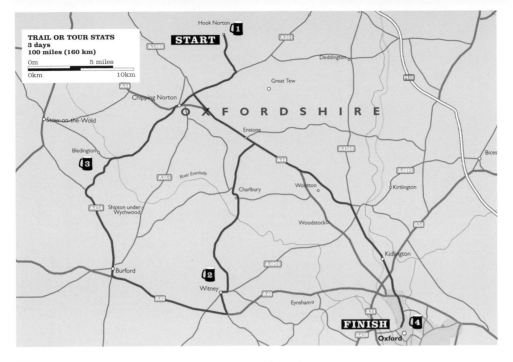

TRAIL OR TOUR STATS
3 days
100 miles (160 km)

0m   5 miles

0km   10km

4 DAY 3: **OXFORD**
The third day of the trail offers a chance to sample some of the fabulous pubs in the historical city of Oxford—a place where good beer, culture, and a convivial atmosphere sit cosily together.

The Bear
Small and friendly, The Bear is on a narrow lane between Christ Church and Oriel colleges. It claims to be the oldest pub in Oxford, and is built on the site of a former bear-fighting pit. The walls are decorated by a collection of 5,000 ties.
6 Alfred Street, Oxford

King's Arms
The King's Arms sits at the end of Broad Street, which is famous for its colleges and bookshops. The large pub is a warren of rooms and is much loved by locals and students.
40 Holywell Street, Oxford

Turf Tavern
Hard to find but worth the search, the Turf Tavern is built on the only remaining part of the city wall. It sells a fabulous collection of British beers. *Bath Place, Holywell, Oxford; for directions go to the pub's website: www.theturftavern.co.uk*

Eagle & Child
Near Oxford's dreaming spires and the Ashmolean museum of art and architecture, the Eagle & Child was a haunt of writers J.R.R. Tolkein and C.S. Lewis, who were part of a literary group in the 1930s and 40s called the *Inklings. 49 St. Giles, Oxford*

189

Hopworks / HUB

USA

944 SE Powell Boulevard
Portland, OR 97202,
www.hopworksbeer.com

Hopworks Urban Brewery is the
first brewery in Portland to offer only
organic beers, part of its commitment
to "green culture." HUB's founder-
brewmaster Christian Ettinger made
Portland's first organic beers.

BREWING SECRET HUB fires its
brewing kettle with bio-diesel fuel.

Velvet ESB
SPECIAL BITTER 5.2% ABV
A session ale by American
standards; rich in caramel, soft
on the palate, with signature
hop character throughout.

Organic IPA
INDIA PALE ALE 6.6% ABV
Fresh hop aromas—pine,
grapefruit, lemon zest. Hop
flavors, bitterness matched
by bright malt character.

Hue

VIETNAM

243 Nguyen Sinh Cung
Hue City,

The Hue Brewery is based in Hue City,
the old capital of Vietnam, on the banks
of the famous Perfume River in central
Vietnam. Carlsberg—which entered
Vietnam in 1993 with the acquisition
of a 60 percent stake in South East
Asia Brewery, based in the north of
the country—now has a 50 percent
share in the Hue Brewery.

Hue
LAGER 5% ABV
A yellow corn color with a thin
white head, and the body seems
somewhat thin too. It is an
easy-drinking beer, without
surprises and a nose with hints
of toast. Not much complexity,
but a refresher nonetheless.

191

Hydes

ENGLAND

46 Moss Lane West,
Manchester, M15 5PH
www.hydesbrewery.com

Hydes is another of those remarkable family-owned breweries that has carved out a niche in its home region. Hydes Original has persevered with the same recipe and exacting standards that were applied on day one—back in 1863. The business continues to face the future with enthusiasm and in confident style.

Hydes Original
BITTER 3.8% ABV
A northwest classic: copper-colored, full-bodied, with a distinctive bittersweet flavor.

Dark Mild
MILD 3.5% ABV
A fruit and malt nose and complex flavorings that meander through berry fruits, malt, and chocolate.

Ilzer Sörgyár

HUNGARY

Ilzer Sörgyár Rt.,
2200, Monor,
www.ilzer.hu

Located 22 miles (35 km) south of
Budapest, this brewery was founded
in the early 1990s. Its range of brews
now includes Alt Bayersicher Dunkel,
a dark wheat beer; Diet, a beer that
is low in sugar; and a kosher beer
called Shalom.

BREWING SECRET Ilzer
developed and brewed the
first Hungarian wheat beer.

Ilzer Hefeweissbier
WHEAT BEER 5% ABV
Cloudy yellow, with a wispy white
head. Hints of banana and spice
give way to a citrussy finish.

Ilzer Roggen Rozs Sör
RYE BEER 4.8% ABV
Hazy to the eye, this is a complex
rye beer of some originality. The
rye imparts rich spice notes.

Iron Hill

USA

Various locations in Delaware
and Pennsylvania,
www.ironhillbrewery.com

Named after a Revolutionary War
landmark in Delaware, the Iron Hill
Brewery & Restaurant chain continues
to grow throughout Delaware and
Pennsylvania, offering a set line-up
at each location but also a range of
specials. Its brewers also package
an Iron Hill Reserve Line in 750 ml
corked bottles for sale at the pubs.

Russian Imperial Stout
IMPERIAL STOUT 9.5% ABV
Rich, dark-chocolate aroma with
supporting coffee notes. Deep
chocolate flavors, balanced by
roasty bitterness.

Pig Iron Porter
PORTER 5.4% ABV
One of their first beers. Roasted
and rich, it's a full-flavored blend
of coffee, prunes, and dark cherries.

Jandelsbrunner

GERMANY

Hauptstr. 17,
94118 Jandelsbrunn,
www.jandelsbrunner.de

The Langs have owned this brewery since
1810. In the 20th century, there was
renewal of equipment such as new filling
machines, and the construction of new
production plants and maturing cellars.

BREWING SECRET In 2004
photovoltaic equipment was
added, to harness the power
of the sun for brewing.

Doppelbock
DOPPELBOCK 8% ABV
The color of this doppelbock is
mahogany, the taste malty,
flowery, and slightly sweet, with
a nice bitter note when finishing.

Ur-Weizen
WHEAT BEER 5.3% ABV
Amber-colored and cloudy from
the yeast, this malty beer tastes
flowery with a mild, sweet finish.

195

Jennings

Cockermouth,
Cumbria, CA13 9NE
www.jenningsbrewery.co.uk

John Jennings had already been
brewing for 46 years when he built his
own brewery in 1874 in the shadow of
Cockermouth Castle. The brewery stands
at the confluence of the Cocker and
Derwent rivers, and has been owned
by Marstons since 2005.

BREWING SECRET Pure
Lakeland water is a key
ingredient in Jennings ales.

Cumberland Ale
BITTER 4% ABV
Florally hoppy, its intense,
full flavor and firm, creamy
body slide into a dry aftertaste.

Sneck Lifter
STRONG BITTER 5.1% ABV
Dark and fascinating, with
complex aromatics, and generous
flavors of fruit and roasted malt.

Jever

GERMANY

Elisabethufer 18,
26441 Jever,
www.jever.de

Jever is one of the top breweries in
Germany. Established 160 years ago,
the company started producing its
export beer in the 1950s. The pilsner
as we know it took off during the
"pils-wave" of the 1960s. Radeberger
bought Jever in 2005.

BREWING SECRET Jever is
famous for making one of the
driest pilsners in existence.

Jever Fun
LOW ALCOHOL 0.25% ABV
Almost alcohol-free, but with
a similar taste to the pilsner.
Hop-bitters and a pilsner taste
pervade this golden beer.

Jever Pilsener
PILSNER 4.8% ABV
The master brewers use a lot of
hops at Jever, and their bitterness
makes this pilsner very dry.

Jolly Pumpkin

USA

3115 Broad Street
Dexter, MI 48130,
www.jollypumpkin.com

Not quite like any other brewery in the
US, Jolly Pumpkin Artisan Ales allows
its beers to develop under the influence
of local wild yeast. All beers are aged
in barrels, and are often blended and
re-fermentated in the bottle to deliver
effervescent beer. Though its output
is small, the brewery has developed
a national following.

Oro de Calabaza
BELGIAN STRONG GOLDEN ALE 8% ABV
Golden and cloudy, tart and spicy,
with orchard fruit and citrus.
Develops with age.

Bam Biere
SAISON 4.5% ABV
The whole exceeds the sum of its
parts in this "farmhouse" ale, from
the hops (billowing head, dry finish)
to the spicy malts.

Jopen

NETHERLANDS

Minckelersweg 2a,
2031 EM Haarlem,
www.jopen.nl

Jopen was founded in 1995 with the
intention of recreating old beer styles
specifically from the Haarlem locale—
once an important brewing center.
This is Holland's only brewery to
concentrate on local recipes, and no
other in the world produces beer in
these styles. A brewpub to showcase
the beers is due to open soon.

Jopen Koyt
GRUIT BEER 8.5% ABV
A recreation of a pre-hop beer
brewed from three grains and
herbs. Fruity, spicy, and delicious.

Jopen Hoppenbier
AMBER ALE 6.5% ABV
Based on a recipe from 1501 using
barley, wheat, and oats; hints of
coriander, ginger, and cloves
complement spicy hops.

Kelham Island

ENGLAND

Sheffield,
outh Yorkshire, S3 8SA
www.kelhambrewery.co.uk

Since Kelham Island opened in 1990,
Sheffield's four large breweries have
closed down, which makes Kelham's
success all the more remarkable.
An astonishing range of awards
has been collected along the way.

BREWING SECRET Pale Rider
and Easy Rider both make
great use of highly fragrant
American hops.

Pale Rider
STRONG BITTER 5.2% ABV
Strong but delicately fruity
multi-award winner, which
profits from an adventurous
use of American hops.

Easy Rider
BITTER 4.3% ABV
A subtle pale ale, its initial crisp
bitterness surrendering only
to a lingering fruity palate.

Keo

CYPRUS

Franklin Roosevelt Ave,
Limassol, 3602
www.keogroup.com

Limassol is the main port and fastest-growing city on the island of Cyprus. It is also home to the Keo Brewery, and no trip to Limassol is complete without visiting the plant, which lies just beyond the Old Port. During the week, there is a daily tour around the brewery—finishing, of course, in the tasting room.

Keo
LAGER 4.5% ABV
A pale lager with a thick head and a sweet malt taste, it is easy on the palate and very drinkable.

Five Beer
LAGER 5% ABV
Deep amber in color, it is rich in malt and low in bitterness. Sweet in the finish.

201

Klein Duimpje

NETHERLANDS

Parallelweg 2,
2182 CP Hillegom,
www.kleinduimpje.nl

This is the brewery of a prize-winning amateur brewer, Erik Bouman, whose porter was chosen as the best of more than 400 entries at the Dutch Homebrewing Championship of 1997. Bouman's competition success prompted him to start brewing professionally. His extensive range of top-fermenting ales includes his celebrated porter.

Hillegoms Tarwe Bier
WITBIER 5.5% ABV
Flavored with coriander and orange peel, this wheat beer is spicy, citric, and just ever so slightly sweet.

Porter
PORTER 5.5% ABV
Espressolike roast malt combines with a chocolate sweetness, backed up with liquorice and toast.

Kona

USA

75-5629 Kuakini Highway
Kailua Kona, HI 97640,
www.konabrewingco.com

Sales are booming everywhere for Kona
Brewing, which offers mainland
drinkers "a pint of paradise." The Big
Island brewery added capacity to meet
growing demand in Hawaii, while sales
in 17 mainland states have increased
even faster. Beers sold on the mainland
are made under contract at Widmer
Brothers in Oregon.

Pipeline Porter
PORTER 5.4% ABV
Brewed with local Kona coffee,
its flavor is well-integrated. Roasty
malt, oily, with chocolate notes.

Fire Rock Pale Ale
PALE ALE 6% ABV
Reddish-orange with slightly
sweet caramel aromas and flavor,
spicy and citric hops are cleverly
integrated and balanced.

König Ludwig

GERMANY

Augsburger Stre. 41,
82256 Fürstenfeldbruck,
www.kaltenberg.de

The history of the Bavarian royal family,
the Wittelsbachers, is closely connected
with the art of beermaking. Today, HRH
Luitpold Prince of Bavaria continues the
family business successfully with his
brands König Ludwig and Kaltenberg.
The latter brand name refers to the
brewery at Kaltenberg Castle.

König Ludwig Dunkel
DUNKEL 5.1% ABV
Amber, with a smooth taste of dark
malt and fine hops, this is the most
popular dunkel in Germany.

König Ludwig Weissbier
WHEAT BEER 5.5% ABV
One of the most popular wheat
beers in Bavaria; cloudy yellow,
with fine hops in the finish. A very
traditional, non-filtered specialty.

De Koninck

BELGIUM

Mechelse Steenweg 291,
B2018 Antwerpen,
www.dekoninck.be

De Koninck is an icon—as is its
main beer. It embodies the town of
Antwerp—whose inhabitants are a
proud lot, and will say so. The amber
"bolleke" (actually the glass) is still
the staple diet in many bars.

BREWING SECRET The draft
version is unpasteurized and
should be tried at its source.

De Koninck

AMBER "SPECIALE BELGE" 5% ABV
Amber malts, residual sugars,
and hops give excellent balance
to a fine ale, with a slight but
distinct sulfury aroma and biscuit
character. The draft version
is particularly good—available
in cask in the UK as well.

Krone Tettnang

GERMANY

Bärenplatz 7,
88069 Tettnang,
www.krone-tettnang.de

Krone Tettnang is a small craft brewery
that has been owned by the Tauscher
family for seven generations. It is a
member of "Brewers with Body and
Soul"—a group of ten small companies
who aim to produce beer "in another,
but traditional, way...."

BREWING SECRET The first
organic beer of the Bodensee
region was made here in 1993.

Keller-Pils
PILSNER 4.7% ABV
The famous first organic beer of the
region. Unfiltered and cloudy, it has
the typical pilsner bitterness of hops
and some sweetness of malt.

Kronenbier
LAGER 4.9% ABV
Richly flavored traditional beer
with the finest possible malt aroma,
and a light finish of fine hops.

Krušovice

CZECH REPUBLIC

270 53 Krušovice 1,
www.pivo-krusovice.cz

When the original owner, Jiří Birka, offered
the brewery for sale in 1581 to Emperor
Rudolf II, the inventory read: "The brewery
kettle is made of stone, so it may be cooked
upon immediately." Those documents
still exist, but Birka would hardly
recognize the highly-mechanized,
industrial brewery today—currently
the nation's fifth-largest producer.

Krušovice Imperial
PREMIUM LAGER 5.5% ABV
A dry straw aroma heightens
a bitter palate, with a floral
hop and malt finish.

Krušovice Dark Beer
DARK BEER 3.8% ABV
Roast malt and caramel generosity
meet earthy and nutty nuances
before a citrus hop finale.

Kuhnhenn

USA

5919 Chicago Road
Warren, MI 48092,
www.kbrewery.com

Brothers Brett and Eric Kuhnhenn
turned the hardware store their father
ran for 35 years into a small brewery,
winery, meadery, and brew-on-premises
(where customers can make their own
beer). The national reputation of
Kuhnhenn shows how word of mouth—
and the Internet—can help small
breweries develop a cult following.

Raspberry Eisbock
EISBOCK 10.6% ABV
A small-run beer. Complex,
rich with raspberries, chocolate,
warming alcohol, and a closing
tartness.

Penetration Porter
PORTER 5.9% ABV
Almost black, with roasted coffee,
chocolate, and dark fruits like
cherry filling the nose and the
mouth. Citrussy hop finish.

Kulmbacher

GERMANY

Lichtenfelser Str. 9,
95326 Kulmbach,
www.kulmbacher.de

The name of Kulmbach, a city in
northern Bavaria, is known to beer-
lovers throughout the world. Its fame
began with the offerings of beer master
Wolfgang Reichel in 1846. Since his
time, many other brands have joined
the company, and production is now
about 70 million gallons (300 million
liters) of beer each year.

Mönchshof Schwarzbier
SCHWARZBIER 4.9% ABV
Dark roasted malts and fine
hops. The deep, dark color and fine
aroma are typical of schwarzbiers.

Kapuziner Weissbier
WHEAT BEER 5.4% ABV
Naturally cloudy, sparkling and
with a sweet and fruity taste;
this unfiltered beer is typical
of the wheat beer style.

Lagunitas

USA

1280 North McDowell Boulevard Petaluma,
CA 94954,
www.lagunitas.com

Always known for its hop-driven beers,
Lagunitas launched a new range in
2006, each one commemorating a
Frank Zappa album and released 40
years after the album of the same
name. Founder Tony Magee obtained
the permission of the Zappa Family
Trust to use the original album art
on the bottle label for these beers.

India Pale Ale
INDIA PALE ALE 5.7% ABV
Brimming with hop character—
orange, grapefruit, peaches,
pine—over malty sweetness.

Kill Ugly Radio
INDIA PALE ALE 7.8% ABV
Only in the US is this an IPA.
Caramel and fermentation fruit
are balanced by spicy, citrussy,
and bitter Northwest hops.

Lakefront

USA

1872 North Commerce Street,
Milwaukee, WI 53212,
www.lakefrontbrewery.com

Lakefront Brewing, known since 1987
for a range of robust beers, recently
moved to the fore in brewing New Grist
gluten-free beer for celiacs who cannot
tolerate the grains traditionally used
in making beer.

BREWING SECRET New Grist is
brewed from sorghum, hops,
water, rice, and gluten-free yeast
grown on molasses.

New Grist
GLUTEN FREE 5% ABV
A tang of citrus zest to start, then
a light palate with hints of fruit.
Mildy astringent and tart.

Riverwest Stein
VIENNA LAGER 6% ABV
Lightly toasted aromas with hints
of caramel. More caramel in the
mouth, and hop citrus fruitiness.
Woody undertones.

Lambrate

ITALY

Via Adelchi 5, 20131 Milano,
www.birrificiolambrate.com

The first (and still the best) brewpub in
Milan, founded in 1996 by brothers Davide
and Giampaolo Sangiorgi and their friend
Fabio Brocca after a visit to 't IJ Brewery
in Amsterdam. They have recently
expanded production, adding some
new, interesting ales. The menu features
some creative beer-influenced dishes,
such as pork cooked in beer mash.

Ghisa
SMOKED ALE 5% ABV
Ebony in color with a "cappuccino"
foam; lighty smoked, easy to drink,
and balanced, with plum notes and
a long, hoppy finish.

Montestella
BLOND ALE 4.9% ABV
Their flagship ale; pale, with fresh
aromas of hay and hops with a long,
dry finish cleansing the palate.

Lao Brewery

LAOS

Km 12 Thadeua Road,
Vientiane,
www.beer-lao.com

The Lao Brewery began production
in 1973 and was originally known as
Brasseries et Glaci è res du Laos. Two
years later, in 1975, it became state
owned. In 2002, Carlsberg and TCC,
a Thai company, each agreed to acquire
a 25 percent stake in Lao Brewery; the
remaining shares are still held by the
Laos government.

Beerlao
LAGER 5% ABV
Described as Asia's best beer,
Beerlao has a pleasant sweetness.
Light bitterness, with hints
of honey.

Beerlao Dark
LAGER 6.5% ABV
Reddish brown, it is full of sweet
toffee and toast flavors. A short
but warming finish.

Lees

ENGLAND

Manchester, M24 2AX
www.jwlees.co.uk

Established by the far-sighted John Lees in 1878, when Manchester was becoming the "workshop of the world," Lees expanded rapidly, matching the growing local thirst. Sixth-generation family members currently run the brewery and pub estate, and they remain faithful to the brewery's maxim: "We think of ourselves as old-fashioned and cutting-edge."

Moonraker
BARLEY WINE 7.5% ABV
Powerfully fruity on a rich roast malt base, with a sweet tendency and dryish finish.

JW Lees Bitter
BITTER 4% ABV
Classic amber-colored northern bitter, with layers of malt in the mouthfeel and a citrus finale.

Lefebvre

BELGIUM

54, Rue du Croly,
B1430 Quenast,
www.brasserielefebvre.be

The first member of the Lefebvre family
to be involved in brewing was Jules in
1876. The brewery is now in the hands of
the sixth generation, with Paul Lefebvre.

BREWING SECRET For a family
brewery, this one is very outward
looking, and now 80 percent of
its beer production is exported.

Floreffe Double
BROWN ABBEY ALE 6.3% ABV
An ale of a chocolatey kind, which
develops madeira and port notes
with a little ageing.

Saison 1900
SAISON 5.2% ABV
One of the few that refers to the
brewery's past; delicate farmyard
and rose water aromas.

215

Left Hand

USA

1265 Boston Avenue
Longmont, CO 80501,
www.lefthandbrewing.com

The company takes its name from
the Arapahoe Chief Niwot, his name
translating as "left hand." Originally
brewing English-style ales, the brewery
merged in 1998 with Tabernash,
known for Bavarian-inspired beers.
Those beers have now been phased
out, but Left Hand continues to
develop a wide range of beer styles
and produces many seasonal brews too.

Milk Stout
MILK STOUT 5.3% ABV
Complex and smooth, chocolate
and burnt toast in the aroma
and flavor constantly balanced
by creamy sweetness.

Blackjack Porter
PORTER 5.2% ABV
Chocolate and liquorice aromas,
medium body, with hints of dark
cherries and a smooth, dry finish.

Leinenkugel's

USA

1 Jefferson Avenue
Chippewa Falls, WI 54729,
www.leinie.com

Since 1988, when Miller Brewing
bought a controlling interest, the
Jacob Leinenkugel Brewing Company
has grown into one of the largest
regional breweries in the country,
distributing in almost every state.

BREWING SECRET The brewery,
founded in 1867, still offers a
range reflecting its German
heritage.

Creamy Dark
US DARK LAGER 4.9% ABV
As creamy as promised, chocolate
with coffee and cream character
and a dryish not-too-bitter finish.

Sunset Wheat
US WHEAT BEER 4.9% ABV
Light but complex beer, almost a
fruit salad of aromas and flavors,
with some wheaty tartness and
coriander spiciness.

217

Liefmans

BELGIUM

Aalststraat 200,
B9700 Oudenaarde,
www.liefmans.be

Although Liefmans parent group went
into receivership at the end 2007, it
looks likely that Duvel Moortgat will
take over, and so the Oudenaarde plant
has a good chance of survival—if, as
before, for lagering purposes only.

BREWING SECRET Liefmans beers
are rare survivors from the once
famous Oudenaards bruin style.

Liefmans Goudenband
OUD BRUIN 8% ABV
A strong interpretation of the style,
its underlying acidity lending the
beer outstanding ageing possibilities.

Liefmans Kriek
OUD BRUIN 6% ABV
The lighter version, refermented with
sour cherries. The rare, un-sweetened
draft version is stellar.

Lindemans

BELGIUM

Lenniksebaan 1479,
B1602 Vlezenbeek,
www.lindemans.be

When considering lambic breweries, we
tend to think about small farm brewers.
Lindemans may seem to fit this bill
at first glance, yet it is also on the
margins of the 10 largest breweries
in Belgium. Its success is owed to
the rather sweetish fruit concoctions
it excels in, with nearly half of the
produce destined for foreign markets.

Lindemans Gueuze Cuvée René
GUEUZE 5% ABV
Initially produced on demand for
export, now this caramel-and-sour-
apple gueuze is fairly common.

Lindemans Kriek Cuvée René
KRIEK 5% ABV
Unfiltered kriek is rare and this
bottled beer is a dry notch above
the draft sweet version.

219

Lion

USA

700 North Pennsylvania Avenue
Wilkes-Barre, PA 18705, www.lionbrewery.
com

The Lion Brewery, founded in 1905,
is a survivor—the last of dozens of
breweries that once operated in
northeastern Pennsylvania. Most
recently the brewery has emphasized
this heritage with its Stegmaier brand
of good-value traditional beers, the
roots of which go back to 1857.

Steg 150
VIENNA LAGER 5.5% ABV
Created to celebrate the brewery's
150th anniversary. Smells like
warm toast, malt-accented, lightly
sweet but smooth, not cloying.

Stegmaier Porter
PORTER 5.5% ABV
Notes of sweet chocolate and ripe
fruit matched with toasty malt
and a coffee-bitter finish.

Lion Brewery

SRI LANKA

254 Colombo Road, Biyagama,
www.lionbeer.com

The company's best-known beer is the
bottle conditioned Lion Stout. The beer
is brewed from British, Czech, and
Danish malts, with Styrian hops
and an English yeast strain. All the
ingredients are transported along
precarious roads to the brewery, located
3,500 ft (1,000 m) above sea level in the
midst of tea plantations.

Lion Stout
STOUT 8% ABV
A world-class beer, with pruney,
mocha aromas and flavors. It has
a tarlike oiliness of body and a
peppery, bitter-chocolate finish.
The alcohol gives it a long
warming finish.

Locher

SWITZERLAND

Industriestrasse 12,
CH - 9050 Appenzell,
www.appenzellerbier.ch

Appenzell is Switzerland's smallest
province (kanton), but the beer
produced by the local brewery
has won it a lot of fame.

BREWING SECRET In the 1990s,
the Locher family found out that
beers brewed on the full moon
ferment more easily; they have,
therefore, created a line of
"Vollmond-brews."

Vollmond
ORGANIC LAGER 5.2% ABV
An aroma of hops and lemon zest;
medium body—chewy; hoppy, but
not excessively bitter.

Holzfass-Bier
LAGER 5.2% ABV
Aromas of sweetcorn, very little
carbonation, and a distinctive note
from the oak in which it is matured.

Lord Nelson

AUSTRALIA

19 Kent Street, The Rocks, Sydney,
New South Wales 2000,
www.lordnelsonbrewery.com

Still going strong after 20-plus years,
Sydney's original modern brewpub
attracts ale lovers to this historic hotel,
which claims to be the city's "oldest
continuously licensed pub." The early
brews were basic malt extract-based
beers, but have evolved into tasty and
complex ales, worthy of this gem of
a watering hole.

Old Admiral
STRONG ALE 6.1% ABV
Dense, malty palate, with plummy
notes, lively bitterness, and a
warming afterglow.

Three Sheets
PALE ALE 4.9% ABV
Malty, fruity aromatics; malt-
accented, with citrus and apricot
hints; well-rounded bitterness.

Lost Abbey

USA

155 Mata Way
San Marcos, CA 92069,
www.lostabbey.com

Port Brewing, born out of a successful chain of brewpubs in the San Diego area, launched the Lost Abbey brand in 2006, and quickly built up devoted following. Brewmaster Tomme Arthur oversees the ageing room, conjuring up what are best thought of as "Wild American" ales—malt-accented beers enhanced by the barrels in which they are matured.

BREWING SECRET The wooden barrels that once held wines and whiskies now nurture wild yeasts.

Red Poppy
SOUR ALE 5.5% ABV
Brown ale with sour cherries, aged in French oak wine barrels for a year. Oaky, with pleasing acidity.

Judgment Day
BELGIAN STRONG DARK ALE 10.5% ABV
Dark and powerful, with profoundly fruity aromas and palate; chocolate and whisky malt undertones.

Löwenbräu

GERMANY

Nymphenburger Str. 7,
80335 München,
www.loewenbraeu.de

Löwenbräu is one of the most famous
brands in the world. The company is
more than 500 years old. In 1948, only
three years after the end of World War
II, Löwenbräu began exporting again:
first to Switzerland, then further afield.
In 1997 there was a marriage between
Löwenbräu and Spatenbräu; today both
are part of the global player InBev.

Löwenbräu Triumphator
DOPPELBOCK 7.6% ABV
Dark brown in color, the
Triumphator has a strong flavor
of malt, but only a subtle aroma
of hops. Sweet.

Löwenbräu Urtyp
EXPORT 5.4% ABV
A balanced flavor with fine aromas
of malt; full-bodied, pleasant, and
fresh, with mild hops in the finish.

Mad River

USA

195 Taylor Way
Blue Lake, CA 95525,
www.madriverbrewing.com

Founder Bob Smith built his brewery
in 1989 using recycled materials,
and has since received many awards
for its waste-reduction programs.
Mad River reuses 98 percent of its
residuals and generates just one yard/
cubic meter of waste a month while
brewing about 250,000 gallons of
beer per year.

Jamaica Red Ale
AMBER ALE 6.6% ABV
First made for the annual reggae
festival. Sweetish nose, with
crystal malts and solid,
refreshing hops.

Steelhead Scotch Porter
PORTER 6.4% ABV
Distinctly a porter, with roasted
malt and a touch of sourness.
Caramel notes and hints of
smoke add complexity.

Magic Hat

USA

5 Bartlett Road
Burlington, VT 05403,
www.magichat.net

Magic Hat's unique and sometimes
outrageous packaging and its "non-
style" beers have brought double-digit
growth year after year. It began in 2008
with construction underway to double
capacity, and plans to push distribution
into the midwest and south.

BREWING SECRET The Orlio
range of beers are certified organic.

#9
PALE ALE 4.6% ABV
Apricot-infused. Subtle stone fruits
on the palate, sometimes buttery
notes. Finishes dry.

Roxy Rolles
AMBER ALE 5.8% ABV
Brewed for the winter season,
rich with caramel and grapefruit
aromas and flavors, balanced by
closing bitterness.

Maisel

GERMANY

Hindenburgstr. 9, 95445 Bayreuth,
www.maisel.com

Hans and Eberhardt Maisel founded
the brewery in the city of Richard
Wagner in 1887. The family decided
to concentrate the production on
wheat beer in 1955, and Maisel
became a trendsetter for this style.

BREWING SECRET Their success
is the result of a high level of ability
in the hand-crafting of beers.

Maisel's Weisse
WHEAT BEER 5.2% ABV
The color is typical for Maisel: a
gleaming red. Fermentation in the
bottle gives the beer fruity notes
and mild nuttiness in the finish.

Maisel's Dampfbier
SPECIAL BEER 4.9% ABV
A very old-fashioned beer: the
mix of different malts gives it
a really special, fine character.

Malt Shovel

AUSTRALIA

99 Pyrmont Bridge Road,
Camperdown, Sydney,
New South Wales 2050,
www.maltshovel.com.au

Positioned as Lion Nathan's craft
brewing arm, the Malt Shovel Brewery
has an impressive portfolio of beer styles
under brewmaster Dr. Charles "Chuck"
Hahn. The brewery's first release in 1998
was Amber Ale, which found ready
acceptance with traditional lager
drinkers. Their James Squire brands
are named after a former convict and
highwayman, who became the colony's
first successful hop grower and brewer.

Malt Shovel India Pale Ale
INDIA PALE ALE 5.6% ABV
Chewy, caramel-tinged maltiness
balanced by robust (dry-hopped)
hop flavor and lingering
bitterness.

James Squire Porter
PORTER 5% ABV
Hints of coffee, dark chocolate, and
dark fruit (plums); a sumptuous
beer, with a smooth finish.

Marston's

ENGLAND

urton upon Trent,
Staffordshire, DE14 2BW
www.marstonsbeercompany.co.uk

The company operates three sites:
the Park Brewery in Wolverhampton,
which brews Banks's, Hanson's, and
Mansfield beers; Jennings Brewery
at Cockermouth in the Lake District,
and the Albion Brewery in Burton upon
Trent. Throughout its long existence it
has acquired several of its competitors.
Then, in 1999, Marston's itself was
taken over by Wolverhampton & Dudley
Breweries, which changed its name
to Marston's PLC in 2007.

Pedigree
BEST BITTER 4.4% ABV
A British institution—sweetly
hop-laden, with the vague sulfur
aroma that's characteristic of
Burton ales.

Old Empire
INDIA PALE ALE 5.7% ABV
A stylish India Pale Ale,
with hop and fruit flavors
and a dry extra-hop finish.

Matilda Bay

AUSTRALIA

130 Stirling Highway, North Fremantle,
Western Australia 6159,
www.matildabay.com.au

Australia's first modern craft brewery
kicked off in Fremantle in 1984, was
acquired by Foster's six years later, and
has been revitalized in recent times.
Original brews such as Redback (a
hefeweizen) and Dogbolter (a dark lager)
have been supplemented with a wide
range of beer styles. Much of the new
direction occurred under the watch
of head brewer Brad Rogers, who has
since left the Foster's fold after 15 years
to embark on a new brewing venture.

Dogbolter
DARK LAGER 5.2% ABV
Roasty, dark chocolate notes;
complex mid-palate; smooth,
coffee-ish finish.

Bohemian Pilsner
CZECH PILSNER 5% ABV
A solid maltiness to the pilsner
is well balanced with a generous
hop bitterness.

231

McAuslan

CANADA

5080 St-Ambroise, Montréal,
Québec, H4C 2G1,
www.mcauslan.com

McAuslan Brewing began in January
of 1989 when its founder Peter
McAuslan decided to turn his
home-brewing hobby into a business.
It quickly established itself as one
of the area's best microbreweries
and was one of the first in Canada
to bottle its products. It produces a
challenging range of seasonal beers.

St-Ambroise Apricot Ale
FRUITY WHEAT BEER 5% ABV
Apricot essence and malted wheat
combine to create an original tasting
beer with a clean, fruit nose.

St-Ambroise Oatmeal Stout
STOUT 5% ABV
Brewed from dark malts and roasted
barley, this stout carries strong
espresso and chocolate notes.

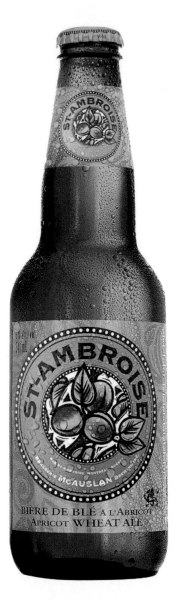

Meantime

ENGLAND

Greenwich, London,
SE7 8RX
www.meantimebrewing.com

Preferring to be known as the brewery
that can't be pigeonholed could be self-
regarding, but the approach of master
brewer Alastair Hook is purposeful—to
demonstrate the exciting flavor potential
that beer has to offer.

BREWING SECRET Research into,
and recreation of, beers from the
past is an abiding passion here,
as exemplified by Meantime's India
Pale Ale.

Meantime Chocolate
SPECIALITY STRONG BEER 6.5% ABV
Complex malt structure, with dark
chocolate releasing vanilla notes to
create a rich, memorable infusion.

India Pale Ale
INDIA PALE ALE 7.5% ABV
Massively hoppy, with herbal,
spice, and grass tiers grasping
the strength of the original IPAs.

Mendocino

USA

South Highway 101
Hopland, CA 13351,
www.mendobrew.com

Mendocino Brewing was one of
the first success stories among US
"boutique" breweries (as they were
called at the time). It opened in
1983 as the Hopland Brewery, having
acquired equipment, the house yeast,
and even a few employees from the
groundbreaking, but by then defunct,
New Albion Brewery.

Red Tail Ale
AMBER ALE 6.1% ABV
An earthy nose includes hints of
orchard fruits. Layers of creamy
malt with notes of liquorice.

Blue Heron
PALE ALE 6.1% ABV
Orange zest and lemon rind to
start, giving way to traditional
biscuity malt and a balanced,
moderate bitterness.

Mettlacher Abteibräu

GERMANY

Bahnhofstr. 32,
66693 Mettlach,
www.abtei-brauerei.de

Mettlacher specializes in natural,
unfiltered beer. Guests can watch the
brewing process from the attached
restaurant. The brewers promote the
beer styles of the region and run
courses on beer production.

BREWING SECRET High-quality
basic products, modern techniques,
and the energy of the brewers
ensure success.

Abtei-Bock
BOCK 6.2% ABV
Strong-roasted bock with obvious
roasty aromas and an even more
intense flavor of fine hops.

Abtei-Josef-Sud
WHEAT BEER 5.1% ABV
The dark amber-colored wheat
beer is sparkling and has typical
aromas from the mash of wheat
and barley malts.

Michigan

USA

1093 Highview Drive
Webberville, MI 48892,
www.michiganbrewing.com

Although Michigan Brewing was one
of the state's biggest breweries before
it bought the defunct Celis brand from
international giant Miller, it is now best
known for that range of beers. Belgian
in style, they were first created by
Pierre Celis (brewer of the original
Hoegaarden beer) after he moved to
Texas. Celis even helped brew the
first batches made in Michigan.

Celis White
WITBIER 4.25% ABV
Cloudy, coriander-spicy, with
citrus all the way through,
wheat tartness, and a soft finish.

Mackinac Pale Ale
PALE ALE 5.5% ABV
The brewery flagship, golden-
orange, not quite pale, with
substantial malt fruitiness. Earthy
and citrussy American hops.

Minhas

USA

1208 14th Avenue
Monroe, WI 53566,
www.minhasbrewery.com

Ravinder Minhas was just 24 years
old when he bought the historic
Joseph Huber Brewery in 2006 to
produce his popular Mountain Creek
brands, already brewed under contract
in Monroe for Canadian distribution.
Minhas Craft Brewery still makes the
Huber brands (dating back to 1843),
Berghoff beers, and a line of grocery
store house label beers as well.

Lazy Mutt
GOLDEN ALE 4.8% ABV
The first released under the Minhas
brand, billed as a "farmhouse ale"
by the brewery but more summer
ale than a *saison*.

Huber Bock
BOCK 5.4% ABV
Toasty and dry, with caramel notes.
Best at Baumgartner's Cheese Store
& Tavern near the brewery.

Minoh AJI

JAPAN

3-19-11 Makiochi, Minoh City,
Osaka 562-0004,
www.minoh-beer.jp

Established by liquor store owner
Masaji Oshita, and run by his
daughters Kaori and Mayuko, Minoh
AJI brewery mostly makes beers
based on American craft beer styles.

BREWING SECRET Among the
more distinctive beers are two that
contain hemp and one that uses
Cabernet Sauvignon grape juice.

Minoh AJI Stout
STOUT 5.5% ABV
Brewed in the Irish style, with lots
of roast flavor and creamy texture,
this stout has a subdued bitterness.

Double IPA
STRONG IPA 9% ABV
Bold and exciting, this strong beer
is only produced as a seasonal so
far, but its popularity may lead to
it becoming available year-round.

238

Moa

NEW ZEALAND

Jacksons Rd, RD3 Blenheim,
www.moabeer.co.nz

Nestled among vines in Marlborough's
wine country is Moa's brewery and
tasting room—the brainchild of
winemaker Josh Scott, who wanted
to make super premium beers with
the winemaking techniques used for
Champagne-style sparkling wines.

BREWING SECRET Moa's
larger 750 ml bottles undergo
the full *méthode traditionelle*
production regime.

Moa Original
BOTTLE-CONDITIONED PILS 5.5% ABV
Extended yeast contact rewards
this delightful dry, crisp pilsner
with a savory toastiness.

Moa Blanc
**BOTTLE-CONDITIONED WHEAT BEER
5.5% ABV**
Dry, crisp, hints of banana and
vanilla; soft natural carbonation.

239

Moctezuma

MEXICO

Monterrey/Veracruz-Llave,
www.femsa.com

Mexico's most innovative brewer,
Moctezuma also has operations in
Brazil and is an important exporter
of beer to the US. It has a powerful
brand portfolio that includes Tecate,
Dos Equis, Sol, Indio, Bohemia, and
Carta Blanc, many of which are sold
in style bars worldwide. Its beers tend
to be smooth, with a spritzy finish.

Dos Equis
VIENNA LAGER 4.8% ABV
Rich and dark red, with chocolate
orange flavors; its warming
sweetness gives way to a long finish.

Sol
LAGER 4.5% ABV
A crisp, light-bodied lager
with a corn syrup aroma.

Biervision Monstein

SWITZERLAND

Monstein, CH-7278 Davos,
www.biervision-monstein.ch

Andreas Aegerter and Christian Ochs
started this village brewery high up in
the mountains near Davos in 2001, along
with 756 small investors (each of them a
devoted customer). They all shared the
vision that there is a market for unusual
beers, as well as beer-related products,
such as cheese crusted with malt and
spirits distilled from beer.

Mungga
KÖLSCH 3.5% ABV
Brewed from organic
Swiss ingredients, Mungga
("groundhog") has aromas
of violets, a dry taste, and
an elegant bitterness.

Royal 11
SPICED BEER 6.5% ABV
Reddish, with pleasant
cherry aromas (from the
local liqueur Röteli); fruity
and only faintly bitter.

Moo Brew

AUSTRALIA

655 Main Road, Berriedale, Hobart,
Tasmania 7011,
www.moobrew.com.au

A stunningly appointed microbrewery,
with commanding views of Derwent
River and Mount Wellington from the
second-story, glass-fronted brewhouse.
An off-shoot of Moorilla Estate winery,
Moo Brew has set a new benchmark
among Australian craft producers,
with slick packaging, uncompromising
beers, and premium pricing.

Moo Brew Pilsner
CZECH PILSNER 5% ABV
Bright, golden, with finely-beaded
bubbles; honey-ish malt character
balanced by herbal hop bitterness.

Moo Brew Pale Ale
US PALE ALE 4.9% ABV
Citrus aromatics; grapefruit notes
dominate mid-palate, rounded out
with substantial, tingling bitter finish.

Moorhouse's

ENGLAND

Burnley,
Lancashire, BB11 5EN
www.moorhouses.co.uk

Mineral water and low-alcohol "hop
bitters" were William Moorhouse's forte.
He started his business in 1865, but his
successors failed to achieve a great deal
in terms of brewing beer until fresh
investment in infrastructure arrived
in 1988. Further improvements and
additions accelerated growth and
helped create the admirable reputation
that Moorhouse ales have today.

Pendle Witches Brew
STRONG BITTER 5.1% ABV
Distinctive and amber-colored,
the beer has a full malty palate
and a resonant fruity hop finale.

Black Cat
MILD 3.4% ABV
Full, dark, and complex, with
distinctive chocolate malt and
liquorice flavors, and a hoppy finish.

Moosehead

CANADA

89 Main Street West, Saint John,
New Brunswick, E2M 3H2,
www.moosehead.ca

Canada's oldest independent brewery
can trace its roots back to 1867, when
Susannah Oland first started brewing
in her Dartmouth, Nova Scotia backyard.
Today, the company is still owned and
operated by the Oland family. Moosehead
has stakes in McAuslan and wholly owns
the Niagara Falls Brewing Company.

Moosehead Lager

LAGER 5% ABV
Pale, staw-colored, clean-tasting
session beer; best drunk cold.

Clancy Amber Ale

ALE 5% ABV
Top-fermented, Clancy's is a
reddish beer, with a distinct malt
aroma and overlays of caramel.

Multi Bintang

INDONESIA

Surabaya, Central Java,
www.multibintang.co.id

Indonesia's largest brewery produces and
markets a range of drinks, including Bir
Bintang, Heineken, Guinness Stout, and
the low alcohol Green Sands. It was
founded in 1929, with Heineken taking
a share of the company in the 1930s.
Though taken over by the Indonesian
government in 1957, Heineken became
involved again in 1967, and today it
is largely owned by them.

Bintang Bir Pilsener
LAGER 4.8% ABV
A fresh malty aroma gives way to
a dry hoppy bitter finish—the beer
clearly draws on its Dutch ancestry.

Bintang Gold
LAGER 4.8% ABV
A slightly darker variation of the
pilsener, brewed to commemorate
the republic's golden anniversary.

New Belgium

USA

500 Linden Street
Fort Collins, CO 80524,
www.newbelgium.com

Jeff Lebesch and Kim Jordan started
out with a system, built to Belgian
specifications, in their cellar in 1991.
They now operate the third largest
craft brewery in the US. Best known
for Fat Tire Ale, the brewery offers
quite a wide range of beers, including
its outstanding Blue Paddle Pilsener.

BREWING SECRET New Belgium
has more capacity for ageing beer
on wood than any brewery other
than Rodenbach Brewery in Belgium.

Fat Tire
AMBER ALE 5.3% ABV
Biscuity, malty nose, with toasted
caramel in the middle and a balanced
finish on the sweet side of dry.

Mothership Wit
WITBIER 4.8% ABV
The brewery's first organic beer.
Fruity and spicy; a creamy texture
and wheat tartness on the tongue.
Refreshing acidity at the finish.

New Glarus

USA

Highway 69
New Glarus, WI 53574,
www.newglarusbrewing.com

In 2008, New Glarus Brewing moved
into a $21 million plant, just outside
a picturesque village settled by Swiss
pioneers in 1845. The attractive
complex is designed to look like
a Wisconsin dairy farm. In 2002 it
was a microbrewery that made 13,700
barrels; by 2007, it had increased
this fivefold. The expansion allowed the
brewery to double production and keep
pace with soaring sales and the demand
for brewmaster Dan Carey's fruit beers
and limited-edition "Unplugged" brews.

Spotted Cow
CREAM ALE 4.8% ABV
Faintly fruity, tasting of fresh
peaches. Pleasantly grainy, light
on the tongue, and refreshing.

Fat Squirrel
BROWN ALE 5.5%
Hazelnuts on the nose, blending
with chocolate and caramel flavors;
nicely balanced by earthy hops.

New Holland

USA

690 Commerce Court
Holland, MI 49423,
www.newhollandbrew.com

New Holland Brewing bottle caps carry
the slogan "Art in Fermented Form,"
which extends from beer to a line of
brandy-flavored vodka, gin, rum, and
other spirits. To keep up with demand
for its assertive beers, the brewery
recently put on line a used copper-
domed, three-vessel brewhouse
acquired from Germany.

The Poet
OATMEAL STOUT 6.5% ABV
Abundant roast, chocolate, and
dark, rummy fruits. Full-bodied
and creamy enough to balance
the coffee start.

Black Tulip
TRIPLE 9% ABV
Floral, with candy and honey
sweetness, and fruity notes.
Sweet but tart in the mouth,
accented by spicy, bitter hops.

North Coast

USA

455 North Main Street
Fort Bragg, CA 95437,
www.northcoastbrewing.com

Since opening in 1988, North Coast
Brewing has cast a larger shadow than
its production levels would suggest.
Though small, it sells beer in 36 states
and exports to Europe and the Pacific
Rim too. Brewmaster Mark Ruedrich
has further extended North Coast's
reputation by exploring beer styles
before many others. Part of the profits
from one, Brother Thelonious, go
to the Thelonious Monk Institute
of Jazz, earning the brewery entry
into many jazz clubs.

Old Rasputin
IMPERIAL STOUT 11.6% ABV
Powerful, but subtle enough for
flavors to emerge—bitter and sweet
chocolate, burnt barley, rum, toffee,
dried dark fruits, and espresso.

Brother Thelonious
BELGIAN STRONG DARK ALE 9.3% ABV
Spicy and candy-sweet aromas, with
dark fruits, notes of banana and
caramelized sugar, almost rummy.

Oakham

ENGLAND

Peterborough,
Cambridgeshire, PE2 7JB
www.oakhamales.com

Impressive growth from modest
homebrew origins has led to the
brewery now occupying its third
site since 1993. The original owner
sold the business on in 1995 but the
early vision and ambitions prevail.

BREWING SECRET American
hop varieties, with powerful
floral characteristics, are a
feature of the range.

Jeffrey Hudson Bitter / JHB
BITTER 3.8% ABV
Dominant citrus fruit hop aroma,
which continues on the palate,
blending into luscious malt flavors.

White Dwarf
WHEAT BEER 4.3% ABV
An English-style wheat beer, with
flinty bitterness that mellows and
reveals fruit nuances.

Okell's

ENGLAND

Douglas,
Isle of Man, IM2 1QG
www.okells.co.uk

Dr. William Okell's steam-powered brewery—which he designed himself in 1874—was regarded as one of the most sophisticated in the world at the time. Okell's new plant, which it moved to in 1994, is the modern equivalent. It is controlled by computers rather than steam, but the passion and commitment to quality beer production remains unaltered.

Doctor Okell's IPA
INDIA PALE ALE 4.4% ABV
Potential sweetness, offset by a high hopping regime for overall roundness, spiced by lemon notes.

Okell's Bitter
BITTER 3.7% ABV
Light colored and complexly flavored, with hints of honey and a long-lingering dry finish.

251

Ommegang

USA

656 County Highway 33
Cooperstown, NY 13326, www.ommegang.
com

Owned by Belgium's Duvel Moortgat,
Brewery Ommegang has brewed ales
in the Belgian tradition since 1997,
selling limited quantities across much
of the US. It hosts one of the nation's
most outstanding beer festivals,
Belgium Comes to Coopers-town,
each summer in the picturesque
brewery grounds outside of town.

Hennepin
SAISON 7.7% ABV
Spicy and peppery throughout.
Yeasty notes, citrus more apparent
on the palate. Tart and dry.

Ommegang Abbey Ale
BELGIAN STRONG DARK ALE 8.5% ABV
The flagship ale, produced in the
spirit of a Christmas beer. Rich
and chocolatey, with underlying
liquorice and festive spices.

Orkney

SCOTLAND

Stromness,
Orkney, KW16 3LT
www.orkneybrewery.co.uk

Commendable ecological awareness
allows the brewery's waste water to
be filtered through two neighboring
lochs that support fish and waterfowl.
It was first set up in 1988, and then
thoroughly modernized in 1994. In
2008, the brewery expanded, adding
a visitor center and shop. Its output
was also increased.

Dark Island
STRONG BITTER 4.6% ABV
Ruby-red and mysterious, with
blackcurrant fruit on the nose
and a full-roasted malt palate.

Skullsplitter
BARLEY WINE 8.5% ABV
Forcefully malty nose; hints
of apple, spicy hop, and some
nut in the complex flavorings.

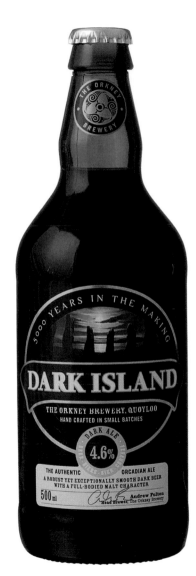

Orval

BELGIUM

2, Abbaye de Notre-Dame d'Orval,
B6823 Villers devant Orval,
www.orval.be

The single Orval Trappist ale is
a symbol of the whole abbey: the
best in early 20th-century Art Nouveau
styling, blending with the medieval
ruins that surround it. The bottle,
glassware, and everything else is
designed with an eye for beauty and
peace. The ruins can be visited, but
alas, not the newly revamped brewery.

Orval

AMBER ALE **6.2%** ABV
An ultra dry ale that owes
a large part of its character
to *Brettanomyces* yeasts, (not
unlike those that define lambic)
and to a high proportion of dry hops.

Ostravar

CZECH REPUBLIC

Hornopolní 57,
728 25 Ostrava 1,
www.ostravar.cz

The Czech Republic's third-largest city
lies closer to Katowice in Poland and
Vienna in Austria than to Prague, and
so prides itself on being "different" to
other Czech breweries. Ostravar beers
reflect this strategic position, and
are carefully considered with local
tradition in mind. It has, however,
been internationally owned (now
by InBev) since 2000.

Ostravar Premium
PREMIUM LAGER 5.1% ABV
A rich head promoting malt and
hop aromas straddle a full-bodied
strong bitter bite.

Ostravar Kelt
STOUT 4.8% ABV
Irish-style stout; pronounced hop
and roasted barley aromas which
continue throughout the palate.

255

Otter Creek

USA

793 Exchange Street
Middlebury, VT 05753,
www.ottercreekbrewing.com

The Wolaver family bought the well-
established Otter Creek Brewery in 2002
in order to make its own organic ales,
which had previously been made under
contract at other breweries. Otter Creek
beers are still produced as well, and the
"World Tour" series includes Otter Mon
(a Jamaican-style stout) and Otteroo (an
Australian-style lager).

Otter Creek Copper Ale
ALTBIER 5.4% ABV
Rich, complex, malty aromas and
flavors, with a sneaky bitterness
that extends the finish.

Wolaver's Oatmeal Stout
OATMEAL STOUT 5.9% ABV
Chocolate and roasted coffee at the
outset, blending with creamy notes
in the mouth. Full-bodied, but
finishing rather dry.

Palmer's

ENGLAND

Bridport,
Dorset, DT6 4JA
www.palmersbrewery.com

Palmer's is able to claim continuous
production on its original site over a
period of more than 200 years. From
the outside it has altered little, but this
is a contemporary brewing operation,
offering a diverse range of ales.

BREWING SECRET Maris Otter
malted barley and Golding hops
combine to give these beers their
fruitiness.

Traditional Best Bitter
BEST BITTER 4.2% ABV
Styled on an India Pale Ale;
deliciously hoppy, with fruit
and malt undercurrents.

Tally Ho!
STRONG BITTER 5.5% ABV
Distinctly nutty and dark,
with full-bodied complexity
emerging slowly, then on
to a lingering afterglow.

Panil (Torrechiara)

ITALY

Strada Pilastro 35/a,
43010 Torrechiara (PR),
www.panilbeer.com

Renzo Losi, a biology graduate, got
his brewing break in 2000, when his
winemaker father gave him permission
to make beer at the family's vineyard
estate, south of Parma.

BREWING SECRET The links
with the family winemaking
tradition are retained in the use of
oak barrels and spumante yeasts.

Panil Barriquée Sour
FLEMISH SOUR RED 8% ABV
The flagship ale, barrel-aged
for three months. Sour, vinous,
and uncompromising.

Divina
WILD BEER 5.5% ABV
Spontaneously fermented by being
left, uncovered, on the back of a
truck in a field overnight. Sweet-
sour, yeasty, and citrussy.

Pelican

USA

33180 Cape Kiwanda Drive
Pacific City, OR 97135,
www.pelicanbrewery.com

Set on the ocean shore, Pelican lies just south of Cape Kiwanda, one of Oregon's most photographed landmarks. Only small quantities are sold outside the pub.

BREWING SECRET Its India Pelican Ale and Doryman's Dark have both been named Grand Champion Beer at the Australian International Beer Awards.

Doryman's Dark Ale
BROWN ALE 5.8% ABV
Malt qualitics—roasted nuts, cocoa, coffee beans, caramel—balanced by Northwest hops.

Tsunami Stout
STOUT 7% ABV
Deep black, with a creamy head. Coffee and chocolate on the nose and palate, rich and almost creamy. Pleasant acidic bite at the end.

259

Pete's

USA

14800 San Pedro Avenue
San Antonio, TX 78232,
www.petes.com

Pete's Brewing was once among the
leading new wave of American beer
companies. Founder Pete Slosburg
sold the business to San Antonio-based
Gambrinus in 1988, and the brand
has not matched the success of other
Gambrinus companies. Brewed under
contract in New York, Pete's is less
widely available today.

Pete's Wicked Ale
BROWN ALE 5.3% ABV
The defining American Brown Ale
when brewed to Slosberg's original
homebrew recipe lost its bite when
the hopping rate was halved.

Wicked Strawberry Blond
FRUIT ALE 5% ABV
More blonde than strawberry, but
berry sweetness begins on the nose
and continues through the finish.

Piccolo Birrificio

ITALY

Via iv Novembre 20,
18035 Apricale (IM),
www.piccolobirrificio.com

This microbrewery, founded in 2005,
is housed in a former olive-oil mill
in the lovely medieval village of
Apricale, near the French border.
Brewer Lorenzo Bottoni produces a
range of fine ales under the brand
name of Nüa ("naked"), including
some amazing brews using unusual
local fruits and plants.

Sesonette
BELGIAN SAISON 6.5% ABV
Matured in Chardonnay barrels
with spices and local chinotto peel
(from a small, bitter citrus fruit).

Chiostro
SPICED ALE 5% ABV
Spiced with *Artemisia absinthium*
(wormwood), then fermented with
Trappist yeasts, giving complex
and unique aromas and flavors.

261

P

Pietra

FRANCE

Route de la Marana,
20600 Furiani,
www.brasseriepietra.com

The first Corsican brewery in history
opened in 1996. Brewers Armelle and
Dominique Sialelli use raw materials
native to the island, such as *maquis*
herbs and chestnut flour, which forms
an ingredient rather than just a
flavoring in their Pietra beer. *Biera
Corsa* has been a great success, both
in Corsica and overseas.

Colomba
WHEAT BEER 5% ABV
Very fresh and sharp, with
unusual aromas of arbutus,
myrtle, and juniper. A
refreshing summer beer.

Pietra
AMBER LAGER 6% ABV
Elegant flavors of toasted malts,
nuttiness, and a slight bitterness.

Pilsner Urquell

CZECH REPUBLIC

U Prazdroje 7, 304 97 Plzeň,
www.pilsner-urquell.cz

The Czechs have blessed us with the
microwave oven, soft contact lenses,
and beer that changed the world.
It was, however, a Bavarian who was
the key player in the Pilsner Urquell
story. As a young brewer, Josef Groll
presented the nation with its first
pilsner on October 4, 1842. This
sensational clear golden beer spread
across Europe like wildfire from its
"original source."

Pilsner Urquell
CLASSIC PILSNER 4.4% ABV
The ideal one-and-a-half inch (35 mm)
tight head leaves a lacing down the
glass with every sip of spiced leaf
and preserved fruit flavors,
developing a sweet malt piquancy
and long, enveloping finish.

263

PRAGUE, CZECH REPUBLIC

The city of Prague is one of the world's greatest beer destinations. And where better to start a beer trail than in the Old Town Square (Staroměstské náměstí), location of the famous 15th-century Astronomical Clock—one of the world's oldest clocks still in working order. Many bars edge the square, each spilling out on to the cobbles with seating and canopies.

1 OLD TOWN SQUARE
Here it is possible to sit outside and savor a beer, while watching the thousands of visitors who now flock to the Czech capital. Displays of folk dancing and music can often be enjoyed here too.

2 U ZLATÉHO TYGRA
One of the Old Town's most atmospheric and oldest bars, U Zlatého Tygra is crowded with small tables, which always seem to be full with locals deep in energetic conversations—so be prepared to stand. It's a favorite of the writer and former Czech President Václav Havel, and President Clinton has also drunk here. The unfiltered Pilsner Urquell is said to be the best in Prague. *Husova 17, Prague*

3 U PINKASŮ
In 1843 U Pinkasů was the first bar in Prague to serve Pilsner Urquell, and it is still available today. The bar was saved from extinction in 2000, when it was extensively refurbished. A more recent refurbishment has opened up more of the building. *Jungmannovo nám, 16/15, Prague*

NOVOMĚSTSKÝ PIVOVAR
4 An Art Deco-style entrance leads visitors down an alleyway of shops to this wood-paneled brewery, pub, and restaurant. Unfiltered light and dark beers are available. The food is unashamedly Czech, with specialties such a goulash, tripe soup, and roast knuckle of pork. *Vodickova 20, Prague*

U FLEKŮ
6 Crowded it may be, a haunt of many tourists it certainly is, but U Flekŭ should not be missed. Brewing began here in 1499, and it is said to be the world's oldest brewpub. It comprises many large rooms, including one for a booming oompah band. It has a small museum and daily brewery tours. The superb house beer is Flekovsky tmavy lezáck, which comes in dark and light versions. *Kremencova 11, Prague*

PIVODUM
5 The Pivodum restaurant and bar is dominated by gleaming coppers. Traditional Czech beers are served, as well as other interesting brews, including a sour cherry beer, a coffee beer, and Samp—a beer champagne. Groups can order eight beers for the price of seven, and they are served in a large giraffelike container. A sample tray of eight beers is available too. *Ječná/Lípová 15, Prague*

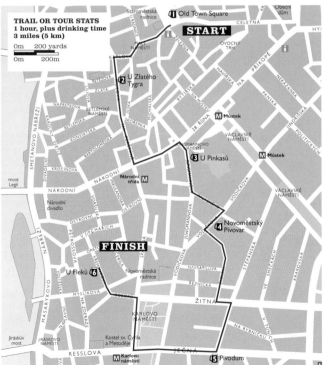

TRAIL OR TOUR STATS
1 hour, plus drinking time
3 miles (5 km)

0m   200 yards
0m   200m

1 Old Town Square
START
2 U Zlatého Tygra
3 U Pinkasů
4 Novoměstský Pivovar
FINISH
6 U Flekŭ
5 Pivodum

De Prael

NETHERLANDS

Helicopterstraat 13-15,
1059 CE Amsterdam,
www.deprael.nl

Set up with the help of government
grants, Amsterdam's smallest brewery
has a workforce made up of recovering
psychiatric patients. The first choice
of name—De Parel ("The Pearl")—had
to be changed when Budels complained
that it infringed on the copyright
of their Parel beer. The solution
was simply to shuffle the letters
of the name around.

Heintje
WITBIER 5.4% ABV
Unspiced, but with prominent
citrus aromas, a touch of fruit,
and an unexpectedly hoppy finish.

Mary
BARLEY WINE 9.6% ABV
Neither malt nor hops dominate
this fruity strong ale, laced with
pepper, toffee, and caramel.

Quilmes

ARGENTINA

Tte. Gral. Juan D. Peron 667 103,
Buenos Aires,
www.quilmes.com.ar

The dominant beer in Argentina,
Quilmes is now part of the InBev
embrace. Like many breweries in
South America, it was begun by a
German, the brewery and malt plant
being founded in the 1880s by Otto
Bemberg. "Quilmes" derives from
an indigenous name for the place
where the brewery is located.

Quilmes Cristal
LAGER 4.9% ABV
Thin and pale, with no aromatic
distractions. Surprisingly
drinkable, though, with
refreshing sweetness.

Quilmes Stout
STOUT 4.8% ABV
Three malts clamor for attention—
but the expected coffee flavors
are overwhelmed by sweetness.

Radegast

CZECH REPUBLIC

39 51 Nošovice,
www.radegast.cz

Radegast, roughly meaning "dear guest," was the Slavic god of fertility and crops, and consequently became proclaimed god of hospitality too. Despite its nominal connections with the dawn of time, the brewery actually began operating only in 1970. It continues to be one of the country's most technologically advanced and best equipped beer producers.

Radegast Original
PILSNER 4% ABV
A light malt and spiced hop nose, malt-sweet flavors and a crisp, grainy bitterness.

Radegast Premium
PREMIUM LAGER 5% ABV
A characteristic herbal hoppy aroma and medium-sweet malt intensity dwell on cereal notes.

Refsvindinge Brewery

DENMARK

Nyborgvej 80,
DK-5853 Ørbæk,
www.bryggerietrefsvindinge.dk

Since 1885, four generations have run
this farmhouse brewery. It was among
the first to brew ales in Denmark and is
credited with developing Danish white beer
(*hvidtøl*) and the old-style smoked "ship's
beer" (*skibsøl*), as well as two varieties of
beer for children (not entirely alcohol free!).

Ale No.16
BROWN ALE 5.7% ABV
Well rounded, typical dark ale
using original English yeast
to produce a sweet, fresh taste.

Mors Stout
PORTER 5.7% ABV
Dark, smooth porter brewed
using malt that has been
roasted with cocoa beans.

Ridna Marka

UKRAINE

71 Mikgorod str.Radomyshl,
www.etalon-beer.com.ua/en

Beermaking in Radomyshl dates from
1886, when this brewery was founded
by the Czech Albrechtam brothers.
They found that the soft water here
was ideal for brewing. The modern
brewery has adapted Bavarian
technology to Ukrainian ingredients.

BREWING SECRET The brewhouse
has been specifically designed
to produce unfiltered, genuine
wheat beers.

Etalon Weissbier
WHEAT BEER 5% ABV
Spicy with a rich, creamy malt note
and a long, quenching flavor and
finish. Hints of bananas and vanilla.

Robinson's

ENGLAND

Stockport,
Cheshire, SK1 1JJ
www.frederic.robinson.co.uk

One of the British Isles' largest
regional breweries, Robinson's began
as the Union Inn in 1838. Sixth-
generation family members are
still in charge of its development,
overseeing huge advances in
brewing and bottling techniques.

BREWING SECRET Tradition
continues here, and the brewery
still uses its surviving 1920s
yeast strain.

Old Tom Strong Ale
BARLEY WINE 8.5% ABV
Full-bodied with an aroma and
flavor alliance of malt, chocolate,
fruit, and port wine.

Unicorn Best Bitter
BEST BITTER 4.2% ABV
Golden, with some spicy hop
and malt on the nose, countered
by a bittersweet release.

Rochefort

BELGIUM

8, Abbaye de Notre Dame de St-Remy,
B5580 Rochefort,
www.trappistes-rochefort.com

Though brewing has been carried out
here since 1900, it is only since 1998 that
Rochefort has used labels on their bottled
beer. Recently, this smallest of the Walloon
Trappist breweries decided to employ a lay
brewmaster, Gumer Santos, to work on
their beer production. Since then, an
amazing new lagering room has begun
taking shape next to the abbey church, and
the few visitors allowed into the abbey are
now proudly shown the new tasting room.

Rochefort 6 (red)
ABBEY ALE 7.5% ABV
Six is a veiled reference to the beer's
density (1060 OG)—and this lightest
and rarest Rochefort enjoys a very
fruity taste.

Rochefort 10 (blue)
ABBEY ALE 11.3% ABV
A superior Trappist ale, with toffee,
chocolate, raisins, and port flavors,
and incomparable complexity.

Rodenbach

BELGIUM

Spanjestraat 133-141,
B8800 Roeselare,
www.rodenbach.be

The Rodenbach family started making
beer in Roeselare in 1821. Now
under the wing of Palm breweries,
Rodenbach has turned resolutely
modern, yet without doing away
with its age-old traditions.

BREWING SECRET The "cathedral"
of wooden fermenters is one of the
most impressive sights in Belgian
brewing.

Rodenbach Classic
OUD BRUIN 5% ABV
Bearing the signs of its mixed
fermentation and wood ageing, it is
vinous in character and refreshing.

Rodenbach Grand Cru
OUD BRUIN 6.5% ABV
A sour beer that has been aged
in barrels: very severe and dry;
one for the connoisseur.

273

Rogue

USA

2320 OSU Drive, Newport,
Oregon 97365,
www.rogueales.com

Rogue Ales has earned an international
reputation for brewing envelope-pushing
beers by creating a well-structured malt
foundation on which to layer massive
hop additions. This approach fostered
the growth of the "Rogue Nation"—loyal
fans who eagerly await the release of
limited-edition beers.

BREWING SECRET Rogue beers
are top-fermented using their own
PacMan yeast which is well suited
for bottle-conditioning.

Shakespeare Stout
STOUT 6% ABV
Dark, roasted chocolate and coffee
mingle with dark fruits and husky
malt. Substantial, balanced hops
and an oily/creamy smooth finish.

Dead Guy Ale
HELLER BOCK 6.6% ABV
Complex, clean malt aromas, rich
and fruity, becoming toastier on
the palate. Bright bitter hops.
Dry and spicy.

Rooster's

ENGLAND

Knaresborough,
North Yorkshire, HG5 8LJ
www.roosters.co.uk

The rules are simple: unconditional care taken in the selection and preparation of raw materials is repaid in flavor. Beer is not an alcoholic commodity to master brewer Sean Franklin, but a serious sensory product, and inventive infusions of lychees, roses, coffee, grapefruit, and chocolate are teased from hop varieties.

Rooster's Yankee
BITTER 4.3% ABV
Aromatic, softly bitter, with aromas of tropical fruit and Muscat grapes lingering alongside tangy malt.

Outlaw Wild Mule
BITTER 3.7% ABV
New Zealand hops create a Sauvignon Blanc wine character in a remarkable and imposing beer.

Rothaus

GERMANY

Badische Staatsbrauerei Rothaus AG,
Rothaus 1, 79865 Grafenhausen-Rothaus,
www.rothaus.de

The Rothaus brewery was
founded in 1791 by the Benedictine
monastery St. Blasien. Today it
is owned by the State of Baden-
Württemberg and is one of the most
profitable regional breweries in
Germany. Although the brewery
does not advertise, the Tannenzäpfle
has become a cult brand in bars
throughout Germany.

Rothaus Tannenzäpfle
PILSNER 5.1% ABV
Tannenzäpfle ("little fir cones")
is a crisp, elegant, well-rounded
pilsner with a slight final
bitterness.

Rothaus Hefeweizen
WHEAT BEER 5.4% ABV
Refreshing top-fermented
beer, with a mild fruity finish.

Rouget de Lisle

FRANCE

Rue des Vernes,
39140 Bletterans,
www.larougetdelisle.com

Opened in 2002, and named after
the locally born composer of *The
Marseillaise*, this brewery develops
up to 15 new beers each year, some
of them using local ingredients
instead of hops for their bitter notes.

BREWING SECRET Among
the ingredients used to replace
hops are wormwood, dandelion,
blackcurrant, and gentian.

Fourche Du Diable
LAGER 5.4% ABV
Amber in color; aromas of spring
flowers and an unusual bitter
note contributed by gentian roots.

Abisinthe
LAGER 6% ABV
Golden and very refreshing, with
aromas of mint, balm, and the
special bitterness of wormwood.

Rulles

BELGIUM

Artisanale de Rulles, 36,
Rue Maurice Grevisse,
B6724 Rulles,
www.larulles.be

Seldom does a brand new brewery
(established only in 2000) meet with
such immediate success. Grégory
Verhelst's brews are mesmerizingly
characterful, and the quality of the
labels is equally amazing.

BREWING SECRET Grégory
Verhelst enlisted the help of the
Orval brewmaster to develop his beers.

La Rulles Triple
BELGIAN PALE STRONG ALE 8.4% ABV
No lack of body here; herbal and
dry-bitterness on the palate, yet
well fermented and strong.

La Rulles Estivale
SEASONAL ALE 5.2% ABV
A refreshing, citrussy, blossom-laden
summer ale—one of the best of its kind.

Russian River

USA

1812 Ferdinand Court
Santa Rosa, CA 95404,
www.russianriverbrewing.com

Owner-brewmaster Vinnie Cilurzo was the first to brew an Imperial India Pale Ale commercially, when he was at Blind Pig Brewing. That beer is now called Pliny the Elder and has become the benchmark for the style. Cilurzo and his wife, Natalie, have built a production brewery separate from their popular downtown brewpub, giving more space for a wider range of barrels and ageing.

Beatification
SOUR ALE 6% ABV
A spontaneously fermented blended beer. Complex, tart mix of fruit and wood. Just right acidity at the finish.

Pliny The Elder
IMPERIAL INDIA PALE ALE 8% ABV
Hoppy aroma, hoppy flavor, and a hoppy bitterness—all supported by a firm malt base.

Saint Arnold

USA

2522 Fairway Park Drive
Houston, TX 77092,
www.saintarnold.com

The oldest surviving and largest craft
brewery in Texas was founded in 1994.
Saint Arnold grew out of its "micro"
status in 2007, although it continues
to sell its beer only within the state
borders. Austrian-born St. Arnold
is one of the patron saints of beer;
the brewery's fermenters are named
after other saints.

Amber
AMBER ALE 5.5% ABV
Caramel and fermentation fruit,
with bright, spicy hops providing
balance. Excellent on cask.

Elissa IPA
INDIA PALE ALE 6.6% ABV
Delightfully hoppy throughout,
brimming with grapefruit character.
Big and juicy, with rich malt to
match the decided bitterness.

Saint Germain

FRANCE

26 route d'Arras,
62160 Aix-Noulette,
www.page24.fr

Two young but experienced brewers
opened this brewery in 2003, with
top-fermentation beers in the *bière
de garde* style. One takes its name
from Saint Hildegard, a German
abbess of the 11th century, who is
often (though incorrectly) credited
with the introduction of hops into
the beermaking process.

Reserve Hildegarde Ambrée
ALE 6.9% ABV
Golden, with a rich nose of cereals,
spices, and honey. Very smooth with
a good bitterness and a long finish.

Page 24 Rhubarbe
ALE 5.9% ABV
Gold in color, with floral aromas.
Very refreshing, with a special
acidity contributed by rhubarb.

Sainte-Hélène

BELGIUM

21, Rue de la Colinne,
B6760 Ethe-Belmont,
www.sainte-helene.be

After a hectic start, this brewery really got going in 2005, when new brewing equipment was installed. The very southwest corner of Belgium seems to be particularly suited to brewing, as new breweries keep popping up there. Ste-Hélène is enthusiastic about promoting its beers, and is a regular at Belgium's many beer festivals.

La Sainte Hélène Ambrée
BELGIAN AMBER STRONG ALE 8.5% ABV
Close in character to the triple, but with more caramel and tobacco notes; well-balanced.

La Djean Triple
BELGIAN AMBER STRONG ALE 9% ABV
A beer with many flavors and impressions, from phenolic to fruity and dry to creamy.

Samuel Adams

USA

30 Germania Street,
Boston, MA 02130
www.samueladams.com

The name Samuel Adams has been
synonymous with craft beer since
Boston Beer Company was one of
just a few specialty beer sellers in
the country. The company launched
the brand in 1984, when it contracted
production to mainstream producers
with excess capacity. Boston Beer
has since purchased some of those
breweries and produces much of its own
beer. The company holds an employees'
homebrew contest each year, with the
winner's beer being sold commercially.

Boston Lager
VIENNA LAGER 4.9% ABV
Complex flowery/piney nose.
Full-bodied, with caramel in the
middle, and a satisfyingly dry finish.

Utopias
STRONG ALE 27% ABV
The strongest beer in the world,
aged in brandy and port barrels.
Serve and sip like a rare cognac.

283

Samuel Smith

ENGLAND

High Street, Tadcaster,
North Yorkshire, LS24 9SB
www.tadcaster.uk.com

Tadcaster has three breweries, with
"Sam's" by far the smallest—although
it can claim to be Yorkshire's oldest.
A plentiful supply of water is drawn
through limestone from its own wells.

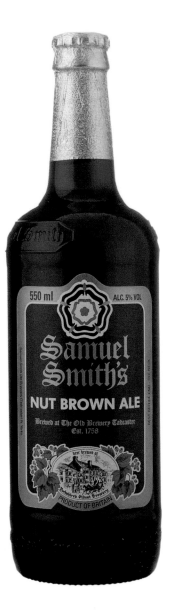

BREWING SECRET Fermentation
takes place in traditional slate
"Yorkshire squares," which
lends distinctive characteristics
to flavor and body.

Nut Brown Ale
BROWN ALE 5% ABV
A hazel-colored specialty,
with a flavor profile of beech
nuts, almonds, and walnuts.

Old Brewery Bitter
BEST BITTER 4% ABV
A typical Northern malty bitter,
with a dash of hop and some
fruit on the palate.

Schlenkerla

GERMANY

Dominikaner Str. 6,
96049 Bamberg,
www.schlenkerla.de

This legendary brewery was known by
1405. Today it is still a relatively small
company, run by a family in its sixth
generation. The so-called "smoked
beer" is a specialty of Bamberg.

BREWING SECRET The distinctive,
smoky aroma of Schlenkerla's beers
comes from beechwood smoke that
pervades the malt as it dries above
the oven.

Aecht Schlenkerla Rauchbier
MÄRZEN 5.1% ABV
A very dark, dry beer. It has smoky
and roasted malt aromas and a finish
of light hops. A pure pleasure.

Rauchbier Urbock
BOCK 6.5% ABV
A traditional dark bock with
Schlenkerla's trademark smoky and
roasty aromas; dry, malty taste and
a good sweetness in the finish.

285

BAMBERG, GERMANY

Can there be a better place in the world to drink beer? This beautiful, baroque island city, on the banks of the Regnitz River and the Main-Donau Canal, is in the Upper Franconia region of Bavaria. It is built on medieval foundations and is home to 70,000 people and 11 breweries. The city is a base for many US army personnel and their families—and they have helped, no doubt, to take the fame of this beer paradise around the world.

1 KLOSTERBRAU
Beer has been brewed at Klosterbrau since 1533. Down a cobbled street, time seems to slip away in this fairytale of a brewery tap. The range includes a schwarzbier, braunbier, weizen, pils, and a bock.
Oberre Muhlbruck 3, Bamberg (www.klosterbraueu.de)

2 OLD TOWN HALL
The river is never far away in Bamberg. The stroll to Brauerei Spezial's passes the spectacular medieval stone-and-timbered Old Town Hall, which seems precariously balanced on the footings of an ancient bridge. Take a moment to admire it before heading on to the Brauerei Spezial's.

3 THE BRAUEREI SPEZIAL'S
The Brauerei Spezial's is very much a locals' bar, decorated with laughter and conversations. Its Specizil Rauchbier has subtle, soft toffee flavors and even a hint of burnt straw. Spezial uses smoked malt in at least four of its other beers. By the bar is a serving hatch, where locals come to fill containers with beer for drinking at home. *Obere Königstrasse 10, Bamberg (www.brauerei-spezial.de)*

4 BRAUEREI FÄSSLA
Directly opposite Brauerei Spezial's is Brauerei Fässla. Brewing started here in 1649. The brewery tap has a comfortable, wood-paneled, country-style room, and above it is a small hotel. The brewery's logo—a dwarf rolling a barrel of beer—decorates the glasses and dark furniture. Fässla's easy-drinking Lagerbier melds malty flavors with a fresh, soft bitterness. *Obere Königsstrasse 19–21, Bamberg (www.faessla.de)*

6 AMBRÄUSIANUM

Opposite Schlenkerla is the Ambräusianum. Here, the brewing vessels can be seen, which makes it seem more like a modern brewpub than one of Bamberg's traditional establishments, and it is a relative newcomer, being open only since 2004. Weekend breakfasts comprise a glass of wheat beer with three locally made Bavarian veal sausages and a pretzel. *Dominikanerstrasse 10, Bamberg (www.ambraeusianum.de)*

5 SCHLENKERLA

Vibrant and friendly, Schlenkerla is Bamberg's best-known bar and restaurant. The warmth of its world-famous rauchbier, with its smoked whiskey and cheese overtones, is as warm as the welcome. Tables are often shared, and the atmosphere is highly convivial. Beer is the social lubricant and the perfect accompaniment to robust Bavarian dishes such as onions stuffed with beery meatballs. *Dominikanerstrasse 6, Bamberg (www.smokebeer.com)*

7 WEINSTUBE PIZZINI

The exterior of the Weinstube Pizzini is somewhat unprepossessing, and do not be deterred by its name—it is neither a wine bar nor a pizza restaurant. Inside this small, brown decorated and time-worn bar, there is a warm-hearted welcome and the opportunity to try Fässla and Spezial beers, as well as a dunkel from Andechser. *Ober Sandstrasse 17, Bamberg*

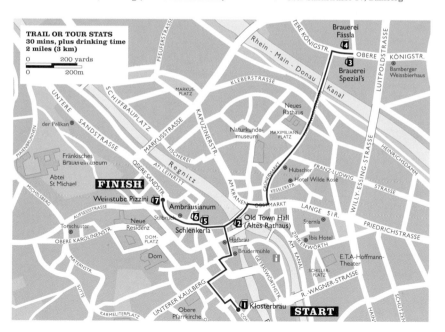

TRAIL OR TOUR STATS
30 mins, plus drinking time
2 miles (3 km)

GREAT BEERS

Schneider

GERMANY

Private Weissbierbrauerei Schneider,
Emil-Ott-Str. 1-5,
93309 Kelheim,
www.schneider-weisse.de

The Schneider brewery has been a
family-owned company since it was
founded. From its original location in
Munich, Schneider moved to Kelheim
after World War II. The former brewery
in central Munich has since become a
world-famous restaurant.

Schneider Weisse Original
WHEAT BEER 5.4% ABV
People call it "liquid amber,"
and they are right: the amber-
mahogany color is beautiful.
Fresh, full-bodied, and with
a light, bitter finish.

Aventinus
STRONG WHEAT BEER 8.2% ABV
Almost black, legendary beer, with
chocolate and dried-fruit aromas;
full-bodied, very thick, and fresh.

Schwechater

AUSTRIA

Mautner Markhof-Strasse 11,
A-2320 Schwechat,
www.schwechater.at

A large brewery that claims to have
brewed the first lager beer in 1840,
though, to be precise, it was the Vienna
lager that was invented here by Anton
Dreher. Production of that beer was
discontinued in the early 20th century.
Nowadays the brewery is part of
Heineken and produces golden lagers.

Schwechater Zwickl
UNFILTERED PILSNER 5.5% ABV
Herbal hop aromas and a hint of
lemon zest. A lot of wheat in the
mash bill. Dry and hoppy finish.

Schwechater Bier
PALE LAGER 5% ABV
Golden color, malty aromas. Full-
bodied with hops being noticeable
from the start to the finish.

289

Sharp's

ENGLAND

Wadebridge, Cornwall,
PL27 6NU
www.sharpsbrewery.co.uk

Facing the Atlantic from the Cornish
coast undoubtedly has an influence,
not only on how the beer is made,
but also on people's objectives and
horizons. Sharp's commendable
approach to sustainable energy and
water recycling is echoed by an
energetic attitude, which is inspiring
for the future of cask ale production.

Doom Bar
BITTER 4% ABV
Spicy resinous hop aromas and
sweet, delicate malts blend with
dried fruit and assertive bitterness.

Atlantic IPA
INDIA PALE ALE 4.8% ABV
Four hop varieties are added at
different stages to create cotton
candy aromas and delicate flavors.

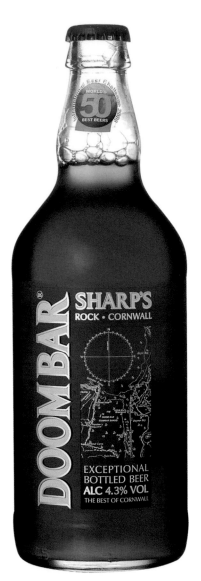

Shepherd Neame

ENGLAND

Faversham,
Kent, ME13 7AX
www.shepherdneame.co.uk

It didn't take 12th-century monks
long to discover that Faversham's
pure spring water could be combined
with locally grown malting barley to
produce particularly fine ale. When
the town's mayor founded a brewery
in 1698 he launched the country's
longest-surviving brewery, which
was by 1864 called Shepherd Neame
still run by the Neame family.

BREWING SECRET The brewery
still makes use of mash tuns
made from Russian teak,
installed in 1914.

Bishop's Finger
STRONG BITTER 5% ABV
Generously fruity, with banana
and pear prominent, a biscuit-rich
maltiness, and dried fruit flavors.

Spitfire
PREMIUM BITTER 4.5% ABV
A underlying deep maltiness is
combined with a subtle hint of
toffee and boldly fruity citrus hops.

Shiga Kogen

JAPAN

1163 Hirao, Yamanouchi-machi, Shimo
Takai-gun Nagano 381-0401,
www.tamamura-honten.co.jp

In September 2004, saké brewer
Tamamura Honten broke a little of
their 200-year tradition and began
brewing beer. Within three years Shiga
Kogen had become one of the most
respected Japanese craft beer brands.
Clear product identity and superior
label designs have contributed to the
beer's popularity.

House DPA / Draft Pale Ale
PALE ALE 8% ABV
American in style, with a brilliant
orange-gold hue, complex floral hop
aroma, and lingering sweetness.

Miyama Blonde
SAISON-LIKE BEER 7% ABV
Made using the Miyama Nishiki
strain of saké rice, along with
European hops and barley. Rich and
interesting, but with a brisk finish.

Shiner

USA

603 Brewery Street
Shiner, TX 77984,
www.shiner.com

Founded in 1909, the Spoetzl Brewery
has ridden the success of Shiner Bock
into national prominence. In 2004 it
began counting down toward its 100th
birthday by releasing a special new
beer every year, each one reflecting a
German heritage that dates back to the
original Shiner Brewing Association.

Shiner Hefeweizen
HEFEWEIZEN 5.3% ABV
Cloudy, brewed in the Bavarian
style with a bit of honey added.
More wheat character than yeast,
with a hint of citrus.

Shiner Bock
US DARK LAGER 4.4% ABV
A dark lager, rather than a true
German bock. Hints of caramel
sweetness. Deliberately low on hops.

Shongweni / Robson's

SOUTH AFRICA

B1 Shongweni Valley, Shongweni,
near Durban, KwaZulu-Natal,
www.shongwenibrewery.com

Shongweni mainly produces bottle-conditioned beers, using the infusion mash technique and fermentation in open-top vessels. All its beers are unfiltered and unpasteurized. The family-owned brewery stands out in a local market dominated by mass-produced lagers. It exports to the UK and elsewhere.

Robson's Durban Pale Ale
INDIA PALE ALE 5.7% ABV
Brewed with Pale malt, and
Cascade and Challenger hops.
Crisp, fruity, and well-balanced.

Robson's East Coast Ale
GOLDEN ALE 4% ABV
A smooth and refreshing golden
ale, made with a single malt
variety along with Brewers Gold
and Challenger hops.

Siebensternbräu

AUSTRIA

Siebensterngasse 19,
A-1070 Vienna,
www.7stern.at

Siebensternbräu was the first brewpub in Austria to brew specialty beers—IPA, chili, and fruit flavored. Owner Sigi Flitter also helped reintroduce many of Austria's indigenous but forgotten beer styles.

BREWING SECRET The range varies with each season, but expect a wheat beer in summer and a smoked in winter.

Rauchbock
SMOKED BOCK 7.9% ABV
Intense smoky nose; full, almost sweet body, with hints of chocolate and liquorice, and a smoky finish.

Prager Dunkles
DARK LAGER 4.5% ABV
While most dark beers in Austria are terribly sweet, this one is dry. Intense toasty notes, very little hop aroma. Roasty finish.

Sierra Nevada

USA

1075 East 20th Street,
Chico, CA 95928,
www.sierranevada.com

Sierra Nevada Brewing has been
introducing beer drinkers to citrussy,
piney Northwest hops since 1981 and
the brewery continues to act as a
matchmaker between beer drinkers and
hops. Sierra Nevada is also an industry
leader in good environmental practice.
It has commissioned the first phase of
one of the country's largest private solar
installations, which will bring it close
to its goal of generating 100 percent
of its energy needs.

Pale Ale
PALE ALE 5.6% ABV
Piney, grapefruity Cascade hops
play against malt fruitiness on
both the nose and the palate.

Bigfoot
BARLEY WINE 9.6% ABV
Earthy and chewy, with prominent
citric hops and whiskeylike rich
malts. Boldly bitter when young.

Silly / Mynsbrug Hen

BELGIUM

2, Ville Basse,
B7830 Silly,
www.silly-beer.com

Established in the 19th century, this
family brewery walks a fine line between
maintaining traditions and employing
technical developments geared toward
satisfying changing market niches.
A *saison* is still produced—bottled and,
better yet, on draft—and they have
recently launched a beer flavored with
rum and named after a regional rock band.

Silly Saison
SAISON 5.2% ABV
Fruity, madeiralike, thin-bodied.
Even when young, this is more
like an oud bruin than a real *saison*.

Scotch Silly
SCOTCH ALE 8% ABV
Scotch ales are a Walloon tradition.
This very malty dark beer is full-
bodied and rich.

Simonds Farsons Cisk

MALTA

The Brewery, Notabile Road,
Mriehel, BKR 01,
www.farsons.com

Wherever the British army went, beer
was soon to follow, and this brewery
was built in lavish Art Deco style at the
end of World War II in 1946. The site
is being redeveloped, with the old brewing
vessels at the heart of a visitor center.

BREWING SECRET It brews the
potent XS (9% ABV) for the
export market.

Farsons Lacto
MILK STOUT 3.8% ABV
Soft on the tongue, this black beer
is a classic milk stout, with lactose
added after fermentation.

Hopleaf Extra
ALE 5% ABV
English malt, along with
Challenger and Target hops,
produce a complex beer with
a refreshing bitter finish.

Sinebrychoff

FINLAND

Oy Sinebrychoff Ab,
Sinebrychoffinaukio 1 PL 87,
FL-04201 Kerava,
www.koff.fi

Sinebrychoff is part of the Carlsberg
Group, and its abbreviated name and
main brand range, Koff, is one of the
most popular in Finland. It is the oldest
Nordic brewery, founded by Russian
Nikolai Sinebrychoff in 1819.

BREWING SECRET
Karhupanimo, their new
microbrewery, is producing a
range of hand-crafted lagers.

Sinebrychoff Porter
IMPERIAL STOUT 7.2% ABV
Robust and brimming with
coffee flavors, this beer has
a long, warming finish.

Karhu III
LAGER 4.6% ABV
Described by the brewer as
"untamed." Full-bodied, with
stronger flavors of hops and
malt than are usual for a lager.

Ska

USA

545 Turner Drive
Durango, CO 81301,
www.skabrewing.com

Bill Graham and Dave Thibodeau
named their brewery for the Jamaican
music they played while homebrewing
in college, reflecting their motto "it
takes characters to brew beer with
character." When they founded Ska
in 1995, they had day jobs and brewed
at night. Now they can't keep up with
the demand for their beers and are
building a new brewery.

Ten Pin Porter
PORTER 5.4% ABV
Chocolate and caramel throughout,
with roasted coffee stronger in
the flavor. Eases into bitterness.

True Blonde
GOLDEN ALE 4.2% ABV
Brewed with honey made just
north of town. Light biscuity
malt, hints of honey, and a
touch of citric hops.

Sleeman

CANADA

551 Clair Road West, Guelph,
Ontario, N1L 1E9,
www.sleeman.com

The Sleeman family started brewing
in Canada in 1834, the year John
Sleeman, an ambitious young brewer
from England, arrived in Ontario. In
1851 he started the first Guelph-based
Sleeman Brewery, making small,
100-barrel batches with local well
water, prized for its purity and
hardness. The company is now
owned by Sapporo.

Honey Brown Lager
LAGER 5% ABV
A refreshingly smooth, full-bodied
lager, with a subtle touch of honey
which creates a slightly sweet finish.

Sleeman Cream Ale
ALE 5% ABV
Designed to combine the refreshing
quality of German lager with the
distinctive taste of English Ale.

GREAT S BEERS

301

Smuttynose

USA

225 Heritage Avenue
Portsmouth, NH 03801,
www.smuttynose.com

Although Smuttynose Brewing has earned a reputation for its carefully balanced offerings, the brewery was also one of the first to embrace "extreme beers," launching a Big Beer Series in 1998. Succeeding on all fronts, it found itself out of room by 2007, and plans to relocate its brewing, still close to Portsmouth.

Shoals Pale Ale
PALE ALE 5% ABV
First made at the Portsmouth pub. Pleasant fruity/biscuit palate gives way to a crisp American hop finish.

Robust Porter
PORTER 5.7% ABV
Rich dark fruits and chocolate, well blended throughout. Rich, roasty flavors leave a strong impression for a medium-strength beer.

Snake River

USA

265 S. Millward Street
Jackson, WY 83001,
www.snakeriverbrewing.com

Located in central Jackson, with a view of Snow King Mountain and standing but a few miles from the Jackson Hole ski resort, Snake River brewpub occupies an old cinder-block warehouse. It has twice won Small Brewery of the Year at the Great American Beer Festival.

Zonker Stout
STOUT 5.8% ABV
Roasted barley sets a bold tone, with chocolate (almost sweet) underneath. Pleasingly dry finish.

Lager
VIENNA LAGER 6% ABV
Golden, with a thick white head. Malt-accented, clean toasted and caramel flavors, drying hop finish.

303

Southampton

USA

40 Bowden Square
Southampton, NY 11968,
www.publick.com

Southampton Publick House's busy
brewmaster, Phil Markowski, routinely
travels to three breweries in New York
State and Pennsylvania to make
Southampton-branded beer. As well
as the eclectic range he's created for
the brewery-restaurant on Long Island,
he also brews specials, packaged in
750ml corked bottles, and oversees
the production of Double White and
Secret Ale. Since early 2008, the
Southampton range of beers has
been marketed by Pabst.

Saison
SAISON 6.5% ABV
An endorsement for "Farmhouse
Ales"—fruity, peppery, slightly
tart, earthy, and refreshing.

Secret Ale
ALTBIER 5.1% ABV
Slightly sweet caramel aromas,
with firm bitterness matching rich
malt on the palate, lasting beyond
the finish.

Starobrno

CZECH REPUBLIC

Hlinky 160/12, 661 47 Brno,
www.starobrno.cz

Brewing around Brno began in
monasteries and convents, notably
those of the Augustinian Brothers
and Cistercian Sisters. The highest
production and technical standards—
features of its Mandell and Huzak
family ownership since 1872—have
earned Starobrno a coveted "Czech
Made" quality certificate. It is now
owned by Dutch firm Heineken.

Starobrno Premium Lager
PREMIUM LAGER 4% ABV
A nose of hay, melon, and
malt, then heightening traces
of caramel on the palate.

Starobrno Rezák
DARK BEER 4% ABV
A deep amber Vienna-style lager
unveiling slight bitter hop and
joyous caramel mouthfuls.

Staropramen

CZECH REPUBLIC

Nádražni 84, 150 54 Prague 5,
www.staropramen.com

Far-sighted developers situated the
Smíchov Brewery in Prague's future
industrial area, where demand for beer
was assured. From the start,
Staropramen—Prague's biggest brewer—
was perceived as a Czech beer for Czech
people, which gave it an advantage
among nationalist-leaning consumers.
Today it is owned by global giant InBev.

Staropramen Dark Beer
DARK BEER 4.5% ABV
Its light body loops around malty
caramel, liquorice, and aniseed
notes to a floral finale.

Staropramen Premium Lager
PREMIUM LAGER 5% ABV
A rich floral bite unveils
a full-bodied satisfier with
a riz ("just right") finish.

St. Austell

ENGLAND

St. Austell,
Cornwall, PL25 4BY
www.staustellbrewery.co.uk

The enterprising spirit that
drove Walter Hicks to mortgage his
farm for £1,500 in 1851 and set up a
brewery remains at the core of today's
business. Many of his descendants are
still involved in the company—in its
estate of 168 pubs and in the brewery,
which produces in excess of 40,000
barrels (6.5 million liters) annually.

Tribute
BITTER 4.2% ABV
Specially grown Cornish Gold barley
delivers a rich biscuit aroma,
tempered by intense fruit flavors.

St. Austell IPA
INDIA PALE ALE 3.4% ABV
Full of flavor and packed with
fresh hoppiness; the rounded
palate arrives with veils of caramel.

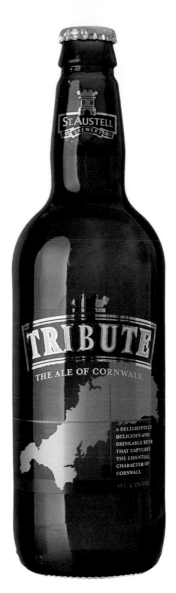

St Christoffel

NETHERLANDS

Metaalweg 10,
6045 JB Roermond,
www.christoffelbier.nl

Operating since 1986, St Christoffel
is one of the oldest Dutch micros,
founded (but no longer run) by
Leo Brand, a member of the Brand
brewing dynasty. It produces the very
best lagers brewed in the Netherlands.

BREWING SECRET The Robertus
beer is a rare example of a
Münchner dark lager that's
true to the Bavarian style.

Christoffel Blond
PILS 6% ABV
Spicy hop flavors burst from
the glass —basil, mint, ginger,
grapefruit, and cloves are all there.

Christoffel Robertus
MÜNCHNER 6% ABV
The nutty flavor of Munich malt
runs right through this beer,
flanked by biscuit, toast, and toffee.

Stiegl

AUSTRIA

Kendlerstrasse 1,
A-5017 Salzburg,
www.stiegl.at

Austria's largest independent brewery
produces Austria's single most
successful beer, Goldbräu. The brewery
itself dates back to 1492 and, over time,
has built up a splendid collection of beer-
related exhibits for the "Brauwelt"—the
largest museum on the continent
entirely devoted to brewing.

Goldbräu
**AUSTRIAN MÄRZEN-TYPE LAGER
4.9% ABV**
Relatively low bitterness and a
hint of malty sweetness in the
aroma and on the palate.

Paracelsus Zwickl
ORGANIC LAGER 5% ABV
Unfiltered, so hazy orange in hue;
aromas of malt and yeast; medium
body and very low bitterness.

Brauhaus Sternen

SWITZERLAND

Hohenzornstrasse 2,
CH-8500 Frauenfeld,
www.brauhaussternen.ch

This is an intriguing brewpub, set
up on the site of the Aktienbrauerei
Frauenfeld, where Martin Wartmann
created Ittinger (now brewed at
Calanda). The present brewery was
built in 2003 with financial help from
many prominent European brewers
eager to see Martin brew interesting
beers, some in limited editions ("Nur
für Freunde"—"for friends only").

Wartmann's Nur Für Freunde No1
BELGIAN DUBBEL 9.6% ABV
Chocolaty, slightly sweet aroma.
Full-bodied and fruity (ripe plums);
very mild bitterness in the finish.

Honey Brown Ale
BROWN ALE 6% ABV
Sweet and fruity. Quite refreshing
for its strength. Very low
bitterness and a hint of
honey in the finish.

Stiftsbrauerei Schlägl

AUSTRIA

Schlägl 1, A-4160 Schlägl,
www.stift-schlaegl.at

The small village of Schlägl, close to
the Czech and Bavarian borders, is
home to the only Austrian brewery
wholly owned by a monastery—in
this case the Premonstratensian
order. In recent years the product
range has grown considerably
and now includes several ales.

Stifter Bier
RED ALE 5.7% ABV
Malty sweetness with a refreshing
fruit (peach and melon) undertone.
Just a faint hint of hops.

Doppelbock
DOPPELBOCK 8.3% ABV
A big, malty nose. Fruity (pears
and apples) and sweet from the
start, but very well-balanced finish.

Stone

USA

1999 Citracado Parkway
Escondido, CA 92029,
www.stonebrew.com

Although some find the "you are not
worthy" campaign, used to promote
Arrogant Bastard Ale, off putting,
CEO Greg Koch's argument in favor
of particularly full-flavored beers is the
opposite of elitist. He doesn't think beer
appreciation takes special skill: "If you
want to turn people on to great beer,
use great beer to do it," he says. That
philosophy has resulted in 30 percent
annual growth year after year, and a
larger brewery, built in 2006.

IPA
INDIA PALE ALE 6.9% ABV
Fruity hop aromas meet firm malt
character at the start, developing
complexity, finishing bitter but
bright.

Imperial Russian Stout
IMPERIAL STOUT 9.4% ABV
Intense, full of chocolate, roasted
coffee, and dark fruits. All balanced
by a brooding bitterness.

Sul Brasileira

BRAZIL

BR 392, Km 05,
Santa Maria—RS, 97000,
http://xingubeer.com

Local folklore says that Sul Brasileira's
Xingu beer is the daughter of a beer
brewed in ancient times by pioneering
Amazonian brewsters. The name
Xinghu (pronounced "shin-goo") is a
tributary of the Amazon River, which
is home to the few surviving cultures
and species of native Amazonian life.

Xingu Black Beer
SCHWARZBIER 4.7% ABV
Dark in color, but light and
sweet to taste. Still in the
glass, its head soon disappears.

Švyturys-Utenos

LITHUANIA

Kuliu Vartu g. 7, Klaipeda,
www.svyturys.lt/en

Brewing began here in 1784, making
this the oldest brewery in Lithuania.
The company has a reputation for the
quality of its beers and has won several
international brewing awards. It is open
to the public for tours twice a week for
groups of five to 25 (via the tourist
office at www.klaipedainfo.lt).

BREWING SECRET All the
employees give their feedback
on each new brew.

Švyturys Ekstra
DORTMUND LAGER 5.2% ABV
Clear and golden, it has a firm
white head, an intense aroma
of hops, and a slight bitterness.

Švyturio
LAGER 5% ABV
Translucent gold in color, it has
a good balance of rich malt and
bitter hops. In Lithuania it's
known simply as "red," due
to its label color.

Teerenpeli

FINLAND

Hämeenkatu 19, Lahti,
www.teerenpeli.com

Teerenpeli operates breweries, bars,
and restaurants in Helsinki, Lahti, and
Tampere. Its first brewery was founded
in 1995. A new brewery and whiskey
distillery opened in 2002, set within
the Restaurant Taivaanranta in Lahti.
Teerenpeli's beers have won medals at
the Helsinki Beer Festival.

Laiskajaakko
DARK LAGER 4.5% ABV
Full-bodied, malty dark lager,
brewed with Crystal 50 and
Black malt, and Hallertau hops.

Onnenpekka
PALE LAGER 4.7% ABV
Golden and refreshing. Made with
Pilsner barley malt from the Lahti
region, and pure water from the
Salpausselkä area.

Terrapin

USA

255 Newton Bridge Road
Athens, GA 30607,
www.terrapinbeer.com

Spike Buckowski and John Cochran
began shipping beer from their own
brewhouse early in 2008, almost six
years after the Terrapin Beer Company
started selling contract-brewed Rye Pale
Ale. That beer was an immediate hit, as
was the Monster Beer Tour, a series of
strong beers released after Georgia
raised its 6 percent ABV cap on beer.

Rye Pale Ale
PALE ALE 5.3% ABV
Rye blends with bright grapefruit,
adds texture to fruit fermentation,
and complements late bitterness.

Wake-n-Bake Coffee
Oatmeal Imperial Stout
IMPERIAL STOUT 8.1% ABV
It's all in the name, along with
chocolate-covered dark fruits.

Theakston

ENGLAND

Masham,
North Yorkshire, HG4 4YD
www.theakstons.co.uk

Ownership battles may have swept in
numerous changes during its 180-year
history but, fortunately today, tradition
survives and thrives. Now returned
to the Theakston family following
Scottish & Newcastle's management,
the company lives up to the name of
its most famous beer—Peculier, a 12th-
century word meaning "particular."

Old Peculier
STRONG BITTER 5.6% ABV
Rich and deep dark ruby in hue,
with a mellow fruit aroma and
a malty, full-bodied flavor.

Black Bull Bitter
BITTER 3.9% ABV
Bright amber colored, with
a crisp, dry palate weaving
through citrus fruit flavors.

317

Thiriez

FRANCE

22 rue de Wormhout,
59470 Esquelbecq,
http://brasseriethiriez.ifrance.com

From working as a manager in a food distribution company, Daniel Thiriez changed his life to become an artisan brewer. He established his brewery on an old farm in Flanders in 1996, and uses traditional brewing methods.

BREWING SECRET Thiriez's unfiltered beers have a second fermentation in the bottle, on their lees.

Étoile Du Nord
BLOND ALE 5.5% ABV
The moment the bottle is opened, an extraordinary smell of fresh hops comes to the nose. The beer's refreshing bitterness is in perfect harmony with its fine malt aromas.

Thornbridge

ENGLAND

Bakewell,
Derbyshire, DE45 1NZ
www.thornbridgebrewery.co.uk

Resounding success has followed
from the brewery's philosophy of
being "never ordinary." While brewing
heritage is of prime importance,
innovation, enthusiasm, experience,
and a commitment to creating new
and exciting recipes have driven the
business since it was established in
2005 in the grounds of Thornbridge
Hall country manor house.

Jaipur
INDIA PALE ALE 5.9% ABV
Tantalizingly complex; emphasis
on citrus hoppiness; its powerful
length develops a bitter finish.

Lord Marples
BITTER 4% ABV
Easy-drinking bitter, with hints
of honey and caramel, and a
long, bitter afterglow.

Three Boys Brewery

NEW ZEALAND

Unit 10, Garlands Rd, Woolston, Christchurch,
www.threeboysbrewery.co.nz

Microbiologist Ralph Bungard employs
a broad range of yeasts to produce tasty
Kiwi interpretations of classic beer styles.
The senior "Boy"—the others are his sons
Marek and Quinn.

BREWING SECRET The brewery's
limited release seasonal brews
include an excellent Oyster Stout
in winter and a fragrant Golden
Ale in summer.

Three Boys Wheat
WITBIER 5% ABV
Plenty of zesty lemon and coriander
notes, with a hint of ginger. A
spritzy and quenching brew.

Three Boys Porter
ROBUST PORTER 5.2% ABV
Rich mocha notes dominate a silky
palate, while heavily roasted grain
and hops compete in the dry finish.

Three Floyds

USA

9750 Indiana Parkway
Munster, IN 46321,
www.threefloyds.com

Beginning with its flagship Alpha King
in 1996, Three Floyds Brewing had
lived by the philosophy of brewmaster
Nick Floyd: "I love the smell of hops
in the morning. It smells like victory."

BREWING SECRET The annual
release of Dark Lord Russian
Imperial Stout sells out in one
day, with customers driving
hundreds of miles to buy it.

Alpha King
PALE ALE 6% ABV
Opens with a rush of citrus fruits.
Firm malt backbone, matched by
hop oils. Prolonged bitterness.

Gumballhead
US WHEAT BEER 4.8% ABV
Citrus and orchard fruits on the
nose, followed by wheat tartness
and hops throughout.

Timmermans

BELGIUM

Kerkstraat 11,
B1701 Itterbeek,
www.anthonymartin.be/Public/

Once a traditional lambic brewery, Timmermans was among the first to habitually mix top-fermented beer into its blends. The brewery has also been eager to produce all kinds of syrup-lambic concoctions, designed to appeal more to the younger generation. Timmermans products, including Tradition, are easily found in Belgian supermarkets.

Tradition Gueuze
GUEUZE 5% ABV
Once known as "Caveau," this beer is a mix of tradition and commercialism, and so are its flavors: more pineapple than citrus, and herbal rather than the typical horse blanket notes.

Timothy Taylor

ENGLAND

Keighley,
West Yorkshire, BD21 1AW
www.timothy-taylor.co.uk

The Taylor family guides the
enterprise, as it has done since
the brewery's inception in 1858.

BREWING SECRET Pure Pennine
water from the brewery's own
spring is a natural companion
to the Golden Promise barley (also
used extensively for malt whiskey);
together, they form the legendary
"Taylor's taste."

Landlord
PREMIUM BITTER 4.3% ABV
Complex hoppy aroma, well-balanced
spice and citrus fruit flavors, tinged
with biscuit malt.

Best Bitter
BEST BITTER 4% ABV
A full measure of maltiness
following citrus fruit, hoppy aromas
define an honest Yorkshire bitter.

Titanic

ENGLAND

Burslem,
Staffordshire, ST6 1JL
www.titanicbrewery.co.uk

What began with brewing for
demonstration purposes on log-fired
Victorian equipment developed into
the production of in excess of 17 million
pints a year. Ecologically friendly
business practices—recycling and
conservation—are a priority. The name
is taken from the world's most famous
passenger ship, whose captain, John
Edward Smith, was born nearby.

Titanic Stout
STOUT 4.5% ABV
Full roast, preserved fruit
aromas; the malt-influenced
palate accentuates more fruit
and liquorice tiers.

Best Bitter
BEST BITTER 3.5% ABV
Straw colored, with a waft
of sulfur in the aroma and
persistent hop flavorings.

Topvar

SLOVAKIA

Krusovska cesta 2092,
Topolcany,
www.topvar.sk

The brewery operates at two sites in
Slovakia: Topolcany and Velký Šariš.
In 2000, the brewery launched a
beer called Brigita, named after
the Slovak finance minister Brigita
Schmögnerovà. A popular beer, it
remained on sale for some time after
her resignation in 2002. The company
is now owned by SABMiller.

Topvar Svetlé
LAGER 5.2% ABV
A sunburst of yellow tones,
with a thin white head. This
beer has an attractive nose,
with plenty of citrus fruit flavors.

Traquair

SCOTLAND

Innerleithen,
Peeblesshire, EH44 6PW
www.traquair.co.uk

The 18th-century brewing equipment
in a house where Bonnie Prince Charlie
once sought refuge remained untouched
until their rediscovery in 1965. Since
then, they have been put to use for
brewing in authentic style.

BREWING SECRET Unusually
in this day and age, Traquair's
beers are fermented in oak
over a seven-day period.

Traquair House Ale
BARLEY WINE 7.2% ABV
A dark and oaky winter brew,
with ripe malt, fruit cake, and
sweet sherry mystique.

Jacobite Ale
BARLEY WINE 8% ABV
Herbal notes from the use of
coriander warm the bittersweet
chocolate and port wine flavors.

La Trappe

NETHERLANDS

Eindhovenseweg 3,
Berkel-Enschot,
www.latrappe.nl

There are just seven genuine Trappist breweries in the world; Koningshoeven (better known as La Trappe) is the only one outside Belgium. The monastery had problems recruiting new monks, and that was one of the factors that prompted the sale of the brewery to Bavaria. Brewing still takes place within the monastery grounds under the supervision of the monks.

La Trappe Witte Trappist
WITBIER 5.5% ABV
Unspiced, but a subtle use of aromatic hops more than compensates, providing delicious citrus and pepper flavors.

La Trappe Tripel
STRONG ALE 8% ABV
Sweetness and fruit give way to coriander, orange, and hop bitterness in this supremely balanced beer.

Tsingtao

CHINA

Hong Kong Road, Central,
Qinqdao, 266071
www.tsingtaobeer.com

The Tsingtao Brewery was founded in
1903 by German settlers in Qingdao.
Today it is part owned by American
giants Anheuser-Busch, which is
currently undertaking a massive
investment in new breweries on the
China mainland. The company runs
over 40 breweries and malt plants
in 18 provinces across China.

Tsingtao
LAGER 4.8% ABV
Crisp, slightly malty flavor and
nutty sweet taste. The color is a
bright yellow; aroma grainy, with
a hint of sweetness. A high level
of carbonation makes it very fizzy.

328

U Medvídků

CZECH REPUBLIC

Na Perštýně 7,
100 01 Prague 1,
www.umedvidku.cz

The restaurant and brewhouse date
back to 1466, though the brewery
has been reinstalled in recent years—
along with extensions and additions to
the pension, which retains its original
Gothic rafters and Renaissance painted
ceilings. This is one of the biggest beer
halls in Prague, and it hosted the city's
first cabaret.

Oldgott Barique Ležák
PILSNER 5.2% ABV
Earthy and melon-fruity aromas,
yeasty characteristics developing
into a roasted malt, caramel infusion.

X-Beer
SPECIALTY BEER 12.6% ABV (VARIABLE)
Matured for 28 weeks in oak vessels
for an elaborate, sweet flavor and
indulgent complexity.

Union

SLOVENIA

Pivovarniška ulica 2,
1000 Ljubljana,
www.pivo-union.si

This brewery was founded in 1864
by the Kozler family, but state-of-the-art
technology makes it one of the most
modern in Slovenia. A fascinating
museum takes visitors through the
brewing process. However, you have
to be there on the first Tuesday
morning of the month to enjoy it.

Union Lager
LAGER 5% ABV
A Slovenian favorite. A sweet,
golden beer, it has corn overtones.

ČRNI Baron / Black Baron
STOUT 5.2% ABV
A dark dessert beer, rich with
caramel notes and aromas; its finish
is warming but could be longer.

United Breweries

INDIA

Bengaluru,
www.theubgroup.com

It is said the company's logo—a Pegasus—once carried a cask of beer between its wings as a gift to the gods. Its Kingfisher brand is the flying leader in India's soaring beer market, and what once was a company that supplied beer to the troops of the British Empire has now acquired a worldwide reputation.

Kingfisher

LAGER 5% ABV
Brewed under license in many countries. It has a crisp taste with a sweetish overtone.

London Pilsner 5.0

LAGER 5% ABV
Thin yellow color, some hop aroma, and a sweetish after taste, it smells of grass.

Upstream

USA

514 South 11th Street
Omaha, NE 68102,
www.upstreambrewing.com

Since opening in 1996 as part of an
"unlinked chain" started by Wynkoop
Brewery, Upstream (a translation of
the Native American name for Omaha)
has gained independence, opened a
second pub, and brewed varieties of
beers not previously found in Nebraska.

BREWING SECRET Developments
include barrel-ageing, and the use
of wild yeast.

Batch 1000 Barley Wine
BARLEY WINE 10.2% ABV
Caramel and vinous on the nose and
palate, blending with lively fruity
esters. Rich, almost chewy, palate.

Grand Cru
BELGIAN STRONG ALE 9% ABV
Aged for a year in oak wine barrels.
Earthy and woody nose, delicate
citrus and honey on the palate,
ultimately balanced.

Vancouver Island

CANADA

2330 Government St, Victoria,
British Colombia, V8T 5G5,
www.vanislandbrewery.com

The inspiration for this company's
formation in 1984 was the absence
of locally made beers on Vancouver
Island. The brewery believes that
brewing should be a perfect blend
of art and science, with no short cuts.

BREWING SECRET Though the
hops and yeast are imported, only
the finest Canadian barley is used.

Hermannator
EISBOCK 9.5% ABV
Brewed and then frozen, it is a
symphony of complex chestnut
colors and spicy flavors.

Hermann's Dark
BAVARIAN LAGER 5.5% ABV
A toasty malt nose with similar
flavors on the palate; takes on
a somewhat nutty character.

Victory

USA

420 Acorn Lane
Downingtown, PA 19335,
www.victorybeer.com

Victory Brewing founders Ron Barchet
and Bill Covaleski—who met on a school
bus in 1973—traveled much of the beer
world, apprenticed in Germany, and
worked in US micro breweries before
starting their own in 1996. The breadth
of their interests is reflected in the
range of their beers.

V

BREWING SECRET Victory has
long-term contracts with German
hop-growers to assure the
availability of authentic
ingredients for their lagers.

Prima Pils
PILSNER 5.3% ABV
Fresh flowery aromas, cookielike
palate, and a solidly bitter-rough
finish. Sturdy yet delicate.

Golden Monkey
TRIPLE 9.5% ABV
Spicy, with hints of banana followed
by light pepper. Candy-sweet on
the palate, with a dry finish.

Wadworth

ENGLAND

Devises,
Wiltshire, SN10 1JW
www.wadworth.co.uk

Established by Henry Wadworth, the
brewery began producing beer in 1875
and was expanded 10 years later into
an impressive, red-brick Victorian
tower brewery. The original open
copper is still operational and wooden
casks are used for local deliveries.
A full-time cooper and a team of dray
horses continue traditional customs.

Wadworth 6X
BEST BITTER 4.3% ABV
A malt and fruit nose, with
restrained hop characteristics
developing an intensity on the
palate.

JEB
STRONG BITTER 4.7% ABV
Aromatic wafts of tropical fruit;
a rich malt mouth with some
nutty sweetness on the palate.

Weitra Bräu

AUSTRIA

Sparkassaplatz 160,
A-3970 Weitra,
www.bierwerkstatt.at

Weitra claims to hold Austria's oldest
brewing privilege, issued in 1321. In
medieval times, most of the buildings
around the town square exercised their
right to brew, now there is only one
brewpub and this brewery left.

BREWING SECRET This organic
specialty brewery, bought by
Zwettler in 2002, still brews
using open fermenters.

Hadmar
ORGANIC VIENNA LAGER 5.2% ABV
Sweet and malty on the nose
and palate; hints of roastyness,
bitterness; variable from batch
to batch.

Weitra Hell
LAGER 5% ABV
Straw colored, with estery aroma
and very little carbonation. Soft on
the palate, with a mild hoppyness.

Wells & Young's

ENGLAND

Bedford, ,
Bedfordshire MK40 4LU
www.charleswells.co.uk
www.youngs.co.uk

A major force in British brewing was created in 2006 from the partnership of London brewer Young's and Bedford-based Charles Wells, two of the most prodigiously accomplished operators in the industry. Wells & Young's cask and bottled ale portfolio is one of the broadest in the brewing sector, particularly after Courage brands—Best Bitter and Directors Bitter—were added in 2007 under an agreement with Scottish & Newcastle.

Wells Bombardier
PREMIUM BITTER 4.3% ABV
Powerful citrus hop aromas meet malt and dried fruit in a richly complex medley.

Young's Bitter
BITTER 3.7% ABV
Well-balanced, with citrus hop notes and enough malt for a flowery and bready finish.

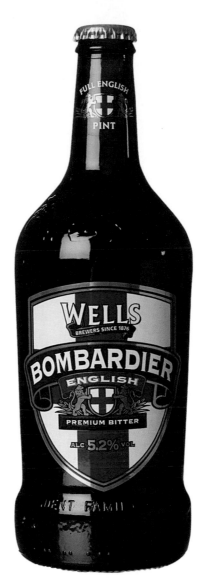

337

Weltenburg

GERMANY

Klosterbaruerei Weltenburg,
Heitzerstr. 2, 93049 Regensburg,
www.weltenburger.de

The Benedictine abbey of Weltenburg
houses the oldest abbey brewery in
the world, founded in 1050. The
location is delightful, close to the
scenic Donau-Durchbruch gorge.
The abbey's restaurant is famous.

BREWING SECRET Despite
its history, the beer is made
with the most advanced
equipment, but is long-matured.

Asam Bock
BOCK 6.9% ABV
A dark mahogany doppelbock.
Very pleasant, it tastes slightly
sweet with nice malty aromas
in the finish.

Anno 1050
EXPORT 5.5% ABV
The abbey's anniversary beer
has a distinctive mix of malt
aromas balanced with hops.

Westmalle

BELGIUM

Antwerpsesteenweg 496,
B2390 Malle,
www.trappistwestmalle.be

Monks started brewing here in 1836,
selling beer at the gate 20 years later.
Today, the abbey operates one of the
world's most modern breweries, hidden
behind the old brewhouse. Westmalle
has come to define abbey ales through
their "Dubbel" and "Tripel" styles. The
"Extra" could be another world classic,
if the monks were to commercialize it.

Westmalle Dubbel
ABBEY ALE 7% ABV
Dark and vinous, with sugar
sweetness coming through;
surprisingly hoppy. A classic.

Westmalle Tripel
ABBEY ALE 9.5% ABV
The dry Champenoise triple that
made all triples blonde. Sweetish
and fruity, with a hoppy finish.

Westvleteren

BELGIUM

Donkerstraat 12,
B8640 Vleteren,
www.sintsixtus.be

The Abbey of St. Sixtus of Westvleteren
is the reclusive star of the beer world.
It sells its beer by telephone reservation
only—unwillingly even—as if to emphasize
that the operation is run by monks who
brew in order to be able to pray, instead
of pray in order to sell. Westvleteren
voluntarily limits production.

BREWING SECRET This is the
only remaining Trappist brewery
that still employs solely in-house
monks.

Westvleteren Blond
ABBEY ALE 5.8% ABV
A blonde ale that starts with a big
grain flavor, followed by very
serious hops; best bitterlike.

Westvleteren ABT 12°
ABBEY ALE 10.2% ABV
A truly massive dark Trappist
ale: chewy like no other beer,
and with a perfect balance
between the sweet and bitter notes.

Wickwar

ENGLAND

Wickwar,
Gloucestershire, GL12 8NB
www.wickwarbrewing.co.uk

A million-pound refurbishment has hoisted Wickwar from microbrewery status to regional heights, increasing its brewing capacity almost fourfold. Beers are matured in below-ground vaults at the former Arnold Perret & Co. Brewery. The export market is an increasing area of interest, with encouraging European sales.

Station Porter
PORTER 6.1% ABV
Richly smooth, with roast coffee, chocolate, and dried fruits combining with complex spiced flavors.

IKB
BEST BITTER 4.7% ABV
Bold in its multi-malt flavors, with rich cherry and plum fruit breaking through.

341

Widmer

USA

929 North Russell
Portland, OR 97227,
www.widmer.com

More than two decades old, the
US-centric Hefeweizen (cloudy but
accented by yeast rather than hops)
that the Widmer brothers basically
invented continues to drive double-digit
growth. Widmer and Redhook have
merged to form a single company
called Craft Breweries Alliance, but
Widmer maintains its own brewery.

Hefeweizen
US HEFEWEIZEN 4.9% ABV
Citrus, particularly lemon zest, is
matched against clean, bready-yet-
tart wheat. Finale of grapefruit.

Snow Plow
MILK STOUT 5.5% ABV
Coffee on the nose becomes
creamier on the palate, roasted
notes blending with rich chocolate.

Williams

SCOTLAND

Alloa,
Clackmannanshire, FK10 1NT
www.heatherale.co.uk

Alloa was once second only to Burton
upon Trent as a brewing center, so it
is encouraging to observe innovative
beer styles still being developed there.
Historic recipes and traditional folklore
methods are skilfully applied.

BREWING SECRET In the Fraoch
Ale, flowering heather is used
instead of hops, reviving an
ancient Celtic recipe.

Fraoch Heather Ale
SPECIALITY BITTER **4.1**% ABV
Abundantly floral and aromatic,
with a spicy mint piquancy, malty
character, and whiff of peat.

Kelpie Seaweed Ale
SPECIALITY BITTER **4.4**% ABV
Organic barley from coastal farms
and bladderwrack seaweed in the
mash produce beguiling flavors.

343

Wismar

GERMANY

Kleine Hohe Str. 15,
23966 Wismar,
www.brauhaus-wismar.de

In the early 15th century, there were
about 180 breweries registered in
Wismar, and the town was well known
all over Europe. The Brauhaus Wismar
was opened in 1452. Today it is the
last brewery remaining in the city
and, since 1995, it has brewed beer
in the style of the medieval Hanseatic
League breweries of northern Europe.

Wismarer Mumme
LAGER 4.8% ABV
An old-fashioned, golden beer with
lovely aromas of malt, light hops on
the tongue, and a long, sweet finish.

Roter Eric
SPECIAL BEER 4.8% ABV
The light red color comes from
the malt; the beer is smooth and
aromatic, with a sweet finish.

Woodforde's

ENGLAND

Woodbastwick, Norwich,
Norfolk, NR13 6SW
www.woodfordes.co.uk

Now on its third site, the brewery
continues to increase production
capacity and to broaden its ambitions.
A tremendous local following has
developed, and the country's top
awards have been accrued—even for
the beermats. Underpinning all this
is high-quality water, which comes
bubbling from an on-site borehole.

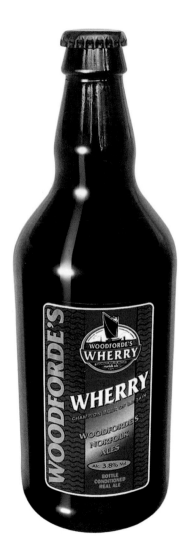

Wherry Best Bitter
BEST BITTER 3.8% ABV
Floral and citrus fruit aromas
unlock a malt-infused middle,
then a sustained finish.

Norfolk Nog
BITTER 4.6% ABV
Deep red, with a roasted malt
background developing through
liquorice nuances and dried fruit.

345

Worthington's White Shield

ENGLAND

Burton upon Trent,
Staffordshire, DE14 1YQ
www.worthingtonswhiteshield.com

The brewery, which dates from 1920,
was reopened in 1995 as a museum
and in order to recreate discontinued
Bass ales, which it has done successfully
under head brewer Steve Wellington.

BREWING SECRET White Shield
became a cult beer for aficionados,
as it is bottled "live" and improves
with age.

White Shield
INDIA PALE ALE 5.6% ABV
Enthusiasts appreciate its hop
attack, its smokiness, treacle toffee
sweetness, dusting of paprika,
and serving of fried banana,
stilton cheese, and sliced apple.

Yanjing

CHINA

9 Shuanghe Road, S
hunyi District, Beijing,
www.yanjing.com.cn

The last remaining large independent
brewer in China, Yanjing often rouses
the attention of the global brewers.
Over the past 25 years Yanjing has
developed into one of the largest beer
producing enterprises in China. It
operates 20 other breweries on the
China mainland, and its output is
predicted to reach 1.1 billion gallons
(5 million kiloliters) by 2010.

Yanjing Beer
LAGER 5% ABV
A sweet, golden syrup nose, it has
overlays of biscuits and corn and
pours a sun burst yellow into a
glass. The brewing water is said to
be from unpolluted mineral water
deep under the Yanshan mountain.

Yoho

JAPAN

1119-1 Otai, Saku City,
Nagano 385-0009,
www.yonasato.com

Yona Yona Ale is perhaps the most popular craft beer in Japan, available in brightly colored cans and on draft all over Japan. While the recipe predates head brewer Toshi Ishii (who previously worked at Stone Brewing in San Diego), he is responsible for their second big success, Tokyo Black, a tasty porter with remarkable flavor and smooth balance.

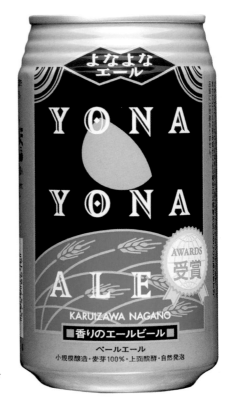

Yona Yona Ale
PALE ALE 5.5% ABV
Square in the American Pale Ale category. Brisk and citrussy, with Cascade hops giving a sharp finish.

Tokyo Black
PORTER 5% ABV
This tasty, roasty beer can best be described as a session porter, with a unique twist. Brewer Ishii recently brewed a batch in England.

Yukon Brewing

CANADA

102A Copper Rd, Whitehorse,
Yukon Y1A 2Z6,
www.yukonbeer.com

Clean water makes clean beer. Yukon
beers start with North America's
cleanest water. Named by some the
Wilderness City, Whitehorse nestles
on the banks of the famous Yukon
River, surrounded by mountains and
clear mountain lakes. Yukon makes
eight beers, including one flavored
with coffee beans.

Lead Dog Ale
ALE 7% ABV
Intricate malt flavors predominate.
Reminiscent of a porter, it has a
slightly darkened, creamy head.

Discovery Ale
PALE ALE 5% ABV
Brewed using honey made from
Fireweed, the official flower of the
Yukon. It finishes dry on the tongue.

GREAT **Y** BEERS

Zagrebacka

CROATIA

Ilica 224, Zagreb,
www.inbev.com

Zagrebacka Pivovara, Croatia's largest
brewer, was established in 1893 and
is now owned by InBev. After years
of falling beer consumption, the market
is now growing again, with domestic
lager brands being the most popular
segment of the market.

BREWING SECRET Double-malted
dark chocolate barley gives the
dark lager its prized aromas,
flavors, and color.

Ožujsko Pivo
LAGER 5.2% ABV
A golden lager, with a deep, white
head. A sweetcorn and malt nose
gives way to a fruity finish.

Tomislav Pivo
DARK LAGER 7% ABV
Croatia's strongest beer, this deep
ruby-red lager has aromas of roasted
malt and coffee, and a dry finish.

350

Žatec

CZECH REPUBLIC

Žižkovo náměstí 81, 438 01 Žatec,
www.zateckypivovar.cz

There is no escaping it in Czech beer
production—every brewery uses the
town's succulent hops, and, as far back
as 1585, Žatec beer was praised for
"its essence, strengths, and virtues."

BREWING SECRET Significant
recent investment has upgraded
its yeast plant, restored open
fermenters, and introduced
state-of-the-art kegging.

Žatec Blue Label
PREMIUM LAGER 4.6% ABV
Hints of grassy hop and sweet
malt, then banana with biscuit
malt on the palate.

Žatec Export
PILSNER 4.6% ABV
Bready aroma with herbal notes,
some sweet malt, delicate spicy hop,
and appropriate apple sourness.

351

Zlatopramen

CZECH REPUBLIC

Dráždanská 80,
400 07 Ústí nad Labem,
www.zlatopramen.cz

Modernization may have accelerated
in recent years, but this brewery's
history is as long as the existence of
brewing privileges. The use of Austrian
Emperor Franz Joseph II's eagle for
its emblem was granted in the early
20th century, while the Zlatopramen
trademark was adopted in 1967. It is
now owned by Drinks Union.

Zlatopramen 11°
PILSNER 4.7% ABV
A faint, earthy hop aroma unfolds
into a full biscuit flavor with a
potent bitterness.

Zlatopramen 11° Dark
DARK BEER 4.6% ABV
Aromatically floral, its sweet
palate, composed from inventive
blends of barley malts, edges
toward toffee.

Zywiec

POLAND

ul. Browarna 88,
34-300 Zywiec,
www.zywiec.com.pl

Established in 1852 by the Hapsburg
family, this brewery fell into state
ownership after World War II, and
was acquired by Heineken in the
mid-1990s. It is home to a lively
brewing museum that takes visitors
right through the brewing process.

BREWING SECRET The Zywiec
Porter uses a recipe from 1881.

Zywiec
LAGER 5.6% ABV
Crisp, gold, and easy-drinking,
with flowery, hoppy aromas,
it is now exported worldwide.

Porter
BALTIC PORTER 9.5% ABV
A dark, strong beer, brewed with
Munich and other special malts
for sweetness and color. Aromatic
hops provide a rich aroma.

Index

This is an index of individual beers only, as the breweries appear in A–Z order in the book.

G R E A T

B E E R S

GREAT BEERS

Acknowledgments

Editor-in-Chief Tim Hampson believes he has one of the best jobs in the world—he is paid to drink beer for a living. A regular broadcaster and writer on beer for many years, he has traveled the world in pursuit of the perfect drink. Chairman of the British Guild of Beer Writers, he wants more people to understand that beer has far greater complexity than wine can ever have. And it is harder to make too. His work appears in *The Telegraph*, *Food & Travel* magazine, *What's Brewing*, *Drinks International*, *Beers of the World*, *American Brewer*, *Brewers Guardian*, and *Morning Advertiser*; he has also appeared on BBC Good Food Live and Sky TV. He is author of *Room at the Inn*.

Contributors
Tim Hampson • Stan Hieronymus • Werner Obalski • Joris Pattyn • Alastair Gilmour • Lorenzo Dabove • Gilbert Delos • Conrad Sidl • Ron Pattinson • Bryan Harrell • Willie Simpson • Geoff Griggs • Laura Stadler-Jensen • Adrian Tierney-Jones

The publishers would like to thank the following people and organizations for their help in the preparation of this book: Beers of Europe, Finn at Utobeer, Jeff at Cracked Kettle, Lithuanian Beer, Belgian Beer Shop, The Grove Tavern, Karen Heptonstall, Malini McCauley, Jennifer Crake at Tourmaline Editions, Florian Bucher, Dorothee Whittaker, Tina Gehrrig, Monika Schlitzer, Ina Melzer at DK Verlag, Dirk Kaufman at DK Inc, Rebecca Carman, Shawn Christopher, Katerina Cerna, Wojciech Kozlowski, Agnes Ordog, Jürgen Scheunemann, Yumi Shigematsu, Diggory Williams, Nora Zimerman. 2010 edition Project Editor Robert Sharman, Project Art Editor Nihal Yesil, Designer Elma Aquino US Editors Jenny Siklós, Shannon Beatty

Images
The publishers would like to thank all the breweries that provided their kind assistance in sending bottles or bottle images to be used within this book and related works.

Thank you to the following companies for their kind permission to reproduce images for features within this book: Pelican 76 (below left); Rogue Brewery 76 (centre left)

Additional studio and location photography by Thameside Media, Quentin Bacon, Jane Ewart, Joe Giacomet, Tim Hampson, Catherine Harries, Alex Havret, Michael Jackson © DK/Michael Jackson, Roger Mapp © Rough Guides, Ian O'Leary © DK, Michael Schönwälder, Mark Thomas © Rough Guides

Maps: Casper Morris, Paul Eames, David Roberts, Iorwerth Walkins

Jacket images: (on front) Hoegaarden Wit, BridgePort India Pale Ale, Guinness Foreign Extra Stout, Starobrno Premium Lager; (on spine) U Medvídků Oldgott Barique Ležák

GREAT BEERS